thai coo

C000225370

delicious easy to make thai recipes

Contents

Text by Sara Burford.
This edition published in 2010 by L&K Designs.
© L&K Designs 2010
PRINTED IN CHINA

Publishers Disclaimer

The recipes contained in this book are passed on in good faith but the publisher cannot be held responsible for any adverse results. Please be aware that certain recipes may contain nuts.

Thai food is a wonderfully unique and inspired style of cuisine, combining vibrant colours, exciting textures, contrasting tastes, tantalizing fragrances and glorious food combinations!

Packed with exotic and delightfully appealing fruits, vegetables, spices and herbs, Thai cooking may seem a little complicated and intimidating to begin with. But have no fear, ingredients that were once difficult to find are now readily available from Asian and Oriental stores and markets, and in more and more instances, from mainstream supermarkets. As for the recipes themselves, they are far from daunting, in fact you'll find them a joy to cook.

The Thai diet is predominantly a very healthy one, with lots of fresh fruit and vegetables, fresh fish, seafood, excellent quality noodles and rice and a healthy balance of meats. Even the desserts are made from healthy ingredients!

It's worth noting that in Thailand, the main meal of the day is presented as a combination of several different dishes, all put out at the same time and centred on rice as the main component.

It's also worth remembering that the Thai palate is accustomed to very hot food, so when you're working with recipes containing chillies or green peppercorns, consider yours and your family's tastes and adjust accordingly!

Thai Cooking is packed full of mouth-watering recipe ideas and easy step-by-step instructions. You'll be able to create fabulous authentic Thai pastes and sauces, tasty snacks and soups, fresh salads and crispy vegetables, superb light meals and main dishes, spicy meats and curries and beautifully delicate desserts.

Providing a must-have list of essential ingredients, this book will make your culinary journey into Thai food even more accessible and hugely enjoyable. Indulge yourself in the culinary delights of Thailand! There is even a space at the back to write your own Thai recipes!

Bamboo Shoots
Popularly used in many Asian cuisines, these are the young, pale-coloured shoots of edible bamboo plants. Easily available in fresh and canned form, they add a slight sweetness and delicately crunchy consistency to Thai dishes.

Bananas
Regularly used in Thai desserts, both normal-sized and the miniature-sized sugar bananas are popularly eaten in Thailand. For optimum sweetness, 'rule-of-thumb' is that the smaller the banana the better.

Bean Sauces
Made from fermented black, yellow or red beans, bean sauces are used to add an extra tang to dishes such as seafood, stir-fries and vegetables. Bean sauces can be found in most supermarkets and Asian and Oriental food stores.

Basil (Holy)
More easily available from Asian/Oriental food stores, holy basil has a slight heat to its taste and is often added at the end of cooking to spicy dishes and fish curries.

Basil (Lemon)
Easily identifiable by its lemon fragrance and sharper taste, lemon basil is used in a variety of dishes, such as salads, curries, seafood and soups.

Basil (Sweet Thai)
A versatile herb, Thai sweet basil has purple stems and provides a unique taste to recipes, popularly used in stir-fries, curry pastes, sauces and also as a garnish.

Chillies (small, medium & long)
There are literally so many kinds of chilli that it would difficult to list them all! A commonly used ingredient in Thai cooking, chillies add different levels of heat and 'zing' to dishes. Rule of thumb is to remember that, generally, the smaller the chilli the hotter the heat! Red chillies are usually less fierce, as ripened chillies lose some of their heat.

The main heat from chillies emanates from the seeds and around the inner membrane, so you may want to remove them if you want a milder flavour. But if you like 'hot-hot-hot!' - then leave them in! Chillies, particularly from exotic locations, come in a range of colours, which as well as adding heat can give a dish a beautiful colourful splash.

Chinese Celery
Compared to regular celery, Chinese celery is darker green in colour and possesses a stronger flavour. Both leaves and stems can be used in cooking. If Chinese celery is unavailable, substituting with regular celery will suffice.

Chinese Chives (flat-leaf/garlic)
Flat-leaf chives have a pronounced garlic odour and a more distinct flavour than regular chives.

Chinese Sausages
Made from seasoned pork, these long and thin sausages are dried and have a hint of sweetness in taste. Popularly used in stir-fries, they can be found in Asian stores and markets.

Coriander Leaves & Root (Cilantro)
A popular herb in a variety of international cuisines, coriander is an essential ingredient in Thai cuisine. The leaves, root and stem of the coriander plant can be used as a distinctive flavouring in a host of dishes. Coriander root is notably only used in Thai cooking, so its inclusion in recipes provides a particularly authentic Thai touch.

Coriander root can be found in Asian and Oriental stores and markets.

Coriander Seeds
Coriander seeds are the dried berries of the coriander plant. Popularly used in Asian cooking, the seeds add a slightly citrus flavour to dishes and pastes.

Coconut Milk & Cream
Made from the pressing of freshly grated coconut, coconut milk and cream are staples in many Thai dishes – giving a distinct sweetness to savoury dishes and popularly being used in delicious Thai desserts. Available in cans, packets and blocks, you can also make your own quite easily.

Coconut (shredded)
A versatile ingredient and available sweetened or unsweetened, shredded coconut can be used in a variety of sweet and savoury dishes, either as a mixed-in ingredient or garnish.

Curry Pastes
Thai curry pastes have a wide range of wonderfully diverse ingredients, including exotic and hot spices, fresh leaves and roots, chillies, coconut milk, ginger, fish sauce, etc. Whether you purchase ready-made pastes or make your own, your taste buds will be treated to some fantastic combinations.

Dried Black Fungus (Cloud Ear Mushrooms)

A popular addition to vegetarian dishes and stir-fries, dried black fungus are slim, ruffle-edged black mushrooms with a delicate taste and crisp texture. They should be soaked in hot water for a little while before using, in order to soften them a little.

Fish Sauce

Although pretty unpleasant to smell, fish sauce is a staple of Thai cooking – and it tastes really goods too. This salty mainstay of Thai cuisine is made from a fermented extract of salted small fish. Due to the fermenting process and the timescales involved, it's infinitely easier to purchase this sauce.

Galangal (fresh)

A relation of ginger but with a more mellow taste, this pink rhizome is another prolifically used ingredient in Thai cooking. Thinly sliced, this fragrant addition is commonly used in curry pastes and soups. Powdered galangal is available, but the taste is diminished in comparison to its fresh counterpart. Fresh galangal can be substituted with a little fresh ginger, if necessary.

Garlic

Another international favourite, garlic is often used in Thai cooking. The strength of the garlic may be an issue, with mild garlic not having as much impact to a dish, so it's good to remember that generally the smaller the garlic, the more prominent the taste.

Ginger

Ginger is a popular and distinctive garnish in Thai cooking with young ginger, (more readily available during the summer), being more suitable.

Green Vegetables

Thai cuisine utilises a wealth of oriental green vegetables in recipes, such as bok choy, Chinese cabbage, choy sum and gai choy… to name a few. Many are now available in mainstream supermarkets, but they will also be readily available in Asian and Oriental stores and markets.

Kaffir Lime
The pared peel of this fruit adds a beautiful zesty flavour to many Thai dishes. If it is unavailable, regular lime zest will be an adequate substitute.

Kaffir Lime Leaf
The leaves of the kaffir lime tree, these fragrant additions to recipes are an important Thai ingredient and are used for their rich, flavourful qualities. The leaves are tough, so aren't pleasant to eat whole – although shredded leaves are often used in soups and ground into curry pastes. Available from Asian or Oriental stores, if not fresh, frozen are better than the dried variety in terms of taste. Regular lime leaves can be used as a substitute.

Lemon Grass
Integral to Thai cuisine, lemon grass has many uses. The green stalks are utilised for things such as flavouring tea and colouring drinks, whilst the white part is commonly used for cooking purposes such as curry pastes and soups. Now more widely available in supermarkets, lemon grass is usually bought in bundles of 4-5 stalks. Follow specific storage instructions to keep fresh lemon grass in prime condition for as long as possible.

Noodles
Noodles are a staple in Thai cooking, being an integral part of a diverse range of delicious and exotic dishes. Noodles come in many different shapes and sizes and are available in both fresh and dried varieties.

Cellophane: Also known as glass noodles, bean thread noodles and vermicelli, (made from mung beans, rather than rice).

Rice: Available in both dried and fresh varieties, rice noodles are available from Asian stores and markets. Dried in long bundles, they can be cut into more user-friendly lengths.

Wheat/Egg (such as Udon): Ordinarily sold in fresh form, these noodles are boiled straight from the packet. They are also sold in dried form.

Pandan (Screwpine Leaf)

Predominantly used to flavour sweet dishes, these long, thin leaves are also used as a popular colouring for drinks and sponges.

Green Papaya (unripe)

Green, unripe papayas, (also referred to as pawpaw), are a delicious and crunchy addition when grated into Thai salads.

Palm Sugar

Packed in both hard and soft forms, (in packed-cake form or in jars), this raw, light brown sugar is widely used in South-East Asia. Soft palm sugar is primarily used in savoury dishes, whereas hard palm sugar is usually used in sweet dishes, often being used to thicken sauces. Locally available in Thailand, they give an authentic taste to Thai dishes, so should be used if possible. If unavailable, brown Demerara sugar may be used as a substitute.

Pepper (white)

White pepper is popularly used in Thai stir-fries, as its taste isn't as overpowering as black pepper.

Peppercorns (green)

Green peppercorns are the undried, immature fruit of the pepper vine. Fresh berries are more flavourful than ones purchased in cans and jars and also it makes them easier to remove from dishes, if the taste is too dominant. Halve the quantity you need if using canned or jarred varieties.

Rice

Rice is without doubt the pivotal component in the Thai diet and is served as the crowning glory of all meals.

Jasmine: With a delicate and flowery fragrance, jasmine rice is the most prominently used in Thailand and is understandably considered to be the best rice to compliment Thai dishes.

Sticky/Glutinous: Regional preferences mean that this rice is more popular in parts of Thailand. Being soaked for many hours before being steamed, its cooked consistency certainly matches its name, sticky!

Rice/cont.

Black: Black rice is another sticky variety of rice, but is principally used in desserts.

Sesame Oil

Made from roasted sesame seeds, sesame oil is often used in the Thai cooking process - providing a rich flavour and distinctive aroma. Use sparingly, so as not to swamp the dish with its flavour.

Shallots

Commonly used in Thai cooking, shallots are easily available and come in a variety of colours. The white part of a spring onion can be used as a substitute.

Soy Sauce

Commonly used to substitute fish sauce in vegetarian side dishes and stir-fries, this popular sauce gives a distinctive and rich taste to its dishes. Available in light and dark varieties, soy sauce is widely available in most stores.

Shrimp (dried)

Pre-soaked or added direct to a dish, dried shrimps are used in a variety of Thai dishes. Dried shrimps can be found in Asian stores and markets.

Ground dried shrimp is the product of grinding dried shrimp, this is also popularly used in Thai cooking.

Shrimp Paste (dried)

Available 'fresh' or in dried form and made from fermented shrimps, this heady and pungent paste is best used in small quantities in sauces and curry pastes. A fabulous source of vitamin B and protein, its use is popular. Available in Oriental stores and markets, shrimp paste is a difficult ingredient to substitute, so if it's not in your cupboard simply exclude it from your recipe.

Tamarind Puree

Bought in either block form or more commonly in jars, tamarind puree has a sour taste and is used in curries and hot and sour soups. When bought in a block, the contents need dilution in water and straining, consequently, buying it in jars is a less labour intensive choice.

Turmeric (fresh)

A popular rhizome used in Thai cuisine, fresh turmeric has a stronger taste than its powdered variety – although both can be used, if fresh turmeric isn't available. Turmeric is often used to neutralise the pungent smell in some fish dishes.

Tapioca Starch

Used to thicken sauces and coat meat before cooking, tapioca starch is made from the cassava root. Similar to cornflour or arrowroot in culinary consistency, these can be used as a substitute.

Tofu (bean curd)

Available in soft and firm forms, both are used in Thai cooking. Highly nutritious and a good source of protein, tofu is a versatile ingredient and absorbs other flavours easily. Soft tofu is generally used as an ingredient in dressings with fresh herbs and in broths, soups and even desserts, whereas firm tofu is used in dishes such as stir-fries and curry dishes.

Pastes
&
Sauces

Chilli & Ginger Sauce

1/2 long red chilli (deseeded & finely chopped)
50g/1/2 cup of fresh root ginger (peeled, grated & squeezed)
1 tbsp light soy sauce
1 tbsp water

1. Squeeze the ginger enough to extract 1 tablespoon of juice. Place the juice in a bowl and add the soy sauce, water and red chilli.

2. Serve or cover and refrigerate until needed.

Chilli Fish Sauce

5 tbsps fish sauce
4 tbsps lemon juice
2-3 large fresh chillies (finely sliced)
1 clove of garlic (crushed)

1. Place all of the ingredients in a bowl and combine well. Transfer to a shallow serving bowl. Serve immediately, or cover and refrigerate until ready to serve.

Serve as an accompaniment.

Chilli & Lime Sauce

4 small red chillies (finely sliced)
2 cloves of garlic (finely chopped)
1 tsp fish sauce
3 tbsps lime juice

Place all of the ingredients in a bowl and whisk together. Serve or cover and refrigerate until needed.

Coconut Milk

150g/2 cups of desiccated coconut
375ml/1 & 2/3 cups of hot water

Coconut Milk/cont.

1. Soak the desiccated coconut in the hot water for 5-6 minutes. Transfer to a blender and blend well.

2. Strain the mixture into a bowl, by squeezing the rich coconut milk through a clean muslin or cotton cloth.

Hot-Shallot Sauce

4 shallots (thinly sliced)
2 tsps ground dried chillies
Juice of 1 1/2 limes
4-6 tbsps fish sauce
2 tsps toasted rice (crushed)

1. Grind the toasted rice in a spice grinder, or with a mortar and pestle.

2. Place the fish sauce, ground toasted rice, lime juice, sliced shallots and dried chillies in a bowl and combine well.

3. Taste and add more fish sauce, if desired. Serve immediately, or cover and refrigerate until ready to serve.

Quick & Easy Peanut Sauce

125g/1 cup of chopped peanuts (crushed)
2 tsps red curry paste
3 tbsps palm sugar
3 tbsps coconut milk
1 tbsp vegetable oil
115ml/1/2 cup of water

1. Heat the vegetable oil in a wok and stir in the curry paste. Cook for 30 seconds and then add the remaining ingredients.

2. Stir all the ingredients together well and reduce the heat to a low setting. Cook for 12-15 minutes, stirring occasionally. Add more water, if required. Transfer to a small bowl and serve with chicken satay.

Satay Sauce

150g/1 cup of roasted peanuts (ground)
250ml/1 cup of coconut milk
1 onion (chopped)
2 cloves of garlic
2 tsps tamarind juice
3 dried red chillies
1 tbsp lemon grass (finely chopped)
1/2 tsp shrimp paste
1/2 tsp ground coriander
1/2 tsp ground cumin
2 coriander roots (chopped)
2 tbsps sugar
2 tsps vegetable oil
Pinch of salt

1. Place the onion, lemon grass, shrimp paste, red chillies, garlic, ground cumin, ground coriander and coriander roots in a food processor and add a little of the coconut milk, in order to moisten the mixture. Blend together.

2. Heat the vegetable oil in a wok and add the blended mixture. Stir-fry the mixture over a gentle heat for a couple of minutes, until the mixture turns a light brownish colour.

3. Add the remaining coconut milk whilst stirring continuously, and combine well. Reduce the heat of the wok to low and add the ground peanuts, stirring them in well to separate.

4. Stir in the tamarind juice, sugar and salt, combining all the ingredients well. Add more coconut milk, if required or simmer gently to reduce down the mixture if needed.

Sesame Oil Sauce

1 tbsp light soy sauce
1 tsp sesame seeds
1/2 tsp sesame oil
1 tbsp vegetable stock

Sesame Oil Sauce/cont.

1. Dry-fry the sesame seeds for 1-2 minutes, until lightly browned. Remove from the pan and leave to cool for 4-5 minutes.

2. Using the back of a spoon, break some of the seeds to release more of the flavour. Place the light soy sauce, sesame oil and vegetable stock in a bowl and stir in the sesame seeds.

Serve or cover and refrigerate until needed.

Spicy Cucumber Relish

1 medium cucumber (finely chopped)
1 small onion (finely chopped)
1 small carrot (finely chopped)
1 red chilli (finely sliced)
115ml/1/2 cup of vinegar
3 tbsp water
225g/1 cup of sugar
1 tsp salt
Fresh coriander leaves (chopped)

1. Place the vinegar, water, salt and sugar in a saucepan and bring to the boil; continue to boil for 1 minute. Remove from the heat.

2. Place the cucumber, carrot and onion in a serving dish and pour over the boiled mixture; just covering all of the vegetables. Leave to cool.

3. Garnish with chopped fresh coriander and serve.

Sweet Chilli Sauce

4 large fresh red chillies
100g/4oz pickled (salted) plums
3 cloves of garlic
115ml/1/2 cup of vinegar
115g/1/2 cup of sugar
1 tsp salt
3-5 tbsps water
Fresh coriander leaves (chopped - to garnish)

1. Place the pickled plums in a saucepan with water and bring to the boil. Boil gently for 5-6 minutes and then drain.

2. Place the boiled plums in a food processor, along with a little plum juice. Blend for 5-8 seconds, until pureed. Transfer into a saucepan and set aside.

3. Place the chillies and garlic in the food processor and blend for about 10 seconds. Transfer to the saucepan with the pureed plums. Stir in the vinegar, sugar and salt.

4. Bring the mixture just to the boil. Reduce the heat and simmer for 8-10 minutes; adding more water when and if required, (depending on preferred consistency). Do not burn or stick to the base of the saucepan. Adjust seasonings, if desired.

5. Transfer to a dish and garnish with chopped coriander leaves.

Thai Green Curry Paste
13-15 fresh green chillies
1 onion (chopped)
10 black peppercorns
4 tbsps lemon grass (chopped)
2 chopped coriander plants (inc. stems & roots)
1 tbsp galangal (soaked in water for 30 minutes)
2 tsps ground cumin
2 tsps ground coriander

Thai Green Curry Paste/cont.

2 bay leaves
2 tsps shrimp paste
3 cloves
1 tsp lime zest (grated)
4 cloves of garlic (finely chopped)
3 tbsps vegetable oil
1 tsp salt

1. Place all of the ingredients in a food processor and blend into a paste.

2. Transfer the required amount to a sealable container and refrigerate, (or use immediately). Freeze the excess, measuring out equal portions, which can be defrosted and used when needed, (usually about 1 1/2 to 2 tbsps per meal for 4).

Thai Red Curry Paste

13-15 dried red chillies
4 cloves
10 black peppercorns
3 bay leaves
1 onion (chopped)
4 cloves of garlic (finely chopped)
1 tsp ground coriander
1 tsp ground nutmeg
1 tsp ground cumin
1 tsp salt
1 tbsp galangal (soaked for 30 mins in hot water & drained)
2 tsp lime zest (chopped)
2 tsp shrimp paste
3 tbsp chopped lemon grass
3 tbsp chopped coriander roots
2 tbsp vegetable oil

1. Grind the dried chillies, peppercorns, ground coriander, cumin, salt, cloves, bay leaves and nutmeg in a spice grinder, or by using a pestle and mortar.

2. Place the remaining ingredients in a food processor and add the freshly ground spice/herb mixture. Blend until a paste-like consistency

3. Transfer the required amount to a sealable container and refrigerate, (or use immediately). Freeze the excess, measuring out equal portions, which can be defrosted and used when needed, (usually about 1 1/2 to 2 tbsps per meal for 4).

Thai Yellow Curry Paste
2 lemon grass stalks (white only, finely sliced)
2 cloves of garlic (chopped)
2-3 long dried red chillies (deseeded & chopped)
3 shallots (chopped)
1 tbsp yellow curry powder
1 tsp ground coriander
1 tsp ground cumin

1. Soak the chopped dried chillies in water for 2-3 minutes, until softened. Drain thoroughly.

2. Place the lemon grass and chillies in a spice grinder and blend to a smooth paste, (alternatively use a pestle and mortar).

Thai Yellow Curry Paste/cont.

3. Add the garlic, shallots, curry powder, coriander and cumin and blend into a smooth paste.

4. Transfer the required amount to a sealable container and refrigerate, (or use immediately). Freeze the excess, measuring out equal portions, which can be defrosted and used when needed, (usually about 1 1/2 to 2 tbsps per meal for 4).

Starters & Soups

Chicken, Bean Sprout & Tofu Soup (Serves 4)

225g/1 cup of minced chicken
150g/1 1/2 cups of 'big head' bean sprouts (washed, tails discarded)
375g/1 & 2/3 cup of tofu (drained & cut into 1 inch cubes)
3 cloves of garlic (finely chopped)
8-10 dried black fungus (soaked for 2 minutes, drained & chopped)
2 tbsps light soy sauce
1 tbsp coriander leaves (finely chopped)
1.9 litres of chicken stock
Ground white pepper (to season)

1. Place the garlic, chicken, dried black fungus and coriander in a bowl and mix together. Using clean fingers, shape the mixture into 1/2 inch balls and set aside.

2. Heat the chicken stock in a saucepan and bring to the boil. Add the soy sauce and reduce the heat down to medium. Carefully, drop the chicken mixture balls into the stock and cook for 3-4 minutes.

3. Add the bean sprouts and tofu cubes and cook for a further 2-3 minutes, making sure that the tofu does not get overcooked and out of shape.

4. Remove from the heat and transfer to a serving bowl. Season with white pepper and serve immediately.

Chicken in Coconut Milk & Hot Chilli Soup (Serves 4)

400g/16oz chicken breasts (skinless & finely sliced)
500ml/2 cups of coconut cream
125ml/1/2 cup of coconut milk
2 tbsps fish sauce
2 tbsps French shallots (chopped)
2 spring onions (chopped)
12 fresh chillies (halved lengthways)
2 stalks lemon grass (white part, peeled & cut into 1 inch pieces)
2 tbsps fresh lime juice
250g/2 cups of straw mushrooms (halved)
1/2 inch of fresh galangal (thinly sliced)

Chicken in Coconut Milk & Hot Chilli Soup/cont.

2 kaffir lime leaves (stemmed)
1 tbsp fresh coriander leaves (chopped)

1. Pour the coconut cream and milk into a saucepan and add the chillies, mushrooms, shallots, galangal and lemon grass. Bring to the boil over a high heat.

2. Reduce the heat and simmer for 4-5 minutes. Add the chicken and continue to simmer gently for 3-4 minutes. Add the kaffir lime leaves and fish sauce.

3. Return to the boil and add half of the fresh coriander leaves. Remove from the heat.

4. Stir in the lime juice and transfer to individual serving bowls. Serve immediately, garnished with the remaining coriander leaves and spring onions.

Chicken Satay (Makes 20)

600g/1 1/3 lbs chicken breasts (cut into chunks)
2 cloves of garlic (chopped)
1 shallot (chopped)
75ml/1/3 cup of chicken stock
2 coriander roots (finely chopped)
100ml unsweetened coconut milk (stirred)
1 tbsp vegetable oil
1/2 inch fresh root ginger (peeled & finely sliced)
1/2 tbsp ground turmeric
1/2 tbsp ground coriander
1/2 tbsp ground cumin
1/2 tsp curry powder
3/4 tbsp light soy sauce
1/2 tbsp palm sugar
20 pre-soaked bamboo skewers

1. Place the garlic, coriander root, shallots and ginger in a food processor and blend into a paste.

2. Place the chicken chunks in a large bowl and add the freshly blended paste. Add the remaining ingredients and using clean hands, mix together thoroughly.

3. Cover and refrigerate for 5-8 hours; turning the chicken occasionally.

4. Thread 2-3 marinated chicken pieces onto the bamboo skewers. Pre-heat the grill to a high heat and line the grill pan with foil.

5. Cook the satay for 6-8 minutes on each side, turning frequently and brushing with more marinade, until cooked through and a little charred.

Serve with peanut sauce.

Coconut & Seafood Soup (Serves 4)
250ml/1 cup of coconut milk
750ml/3 & 1/3 cups of fish stock
300g/11oz prepared squid
350g/13oz raw large prawns (peeled & deveined)
3 tbsps Thai green curry paste
2-3 tbsps Thai fish sauce
4 thin slices of fresh root ginger
4 shallots (chopped)
3 kaffir lime leaves (shredded)
2 lemon grass stalks (chopped)
25g/1oz garlic chives (chopped)
1 tbsp fresh coriander leaves (stalks removed & reserved)
Squeeze of lime juice
1 tsp sunflower oil
Salt & black pepper (to season)

1. Pour the fish stock into a large saucepan and add the lemon grass, ginger slices, coriander stalks, half of the shredded kaffir lime leaves and half of the chopped garlic chives. Bring to the boil.

2. Reduce the heat, cover and simmer gently for 20 minutes. Remove from the heat and strain the liquid stock into a large bowl. Discard the strained ingredients.

Coconut & Seafood Soup/cont.

3. In another large saucepan heat the sunflower oil and add the shallots. Cook for 8-10 minutes over a medium heat, until lightly brown.

4. Stir in the strained stock, 2 tablespoons of fish sauce, the remaining kaffir lime leaves and coconut milk. Heat until just boiling, reduce the heat and simmer gently for 8-10 minutes.

5. Stir in the prawns and curry paste and cook gently for 3 minutes. Add the squid and cook for a further 2-3 minutes.

6. Add the lime juice and season with salt and black pepper, according to taste. Add more fish sauce, if desired.

7. Stir in the remaining garlic chives and coriander leaves. Serve immediately in individual serving bowls.

Garlic Prawns (Serves 6)

750g/1 lb 11oz uncooked medium prawns (shelled & deveined)
7 cloves of garlic (chopped)
3 tbsps vegetable stock
1 1/2 tbsps oyster sauce
20 coriander roots (chopped)
13 black peppercorns
1 1/2 tbsps light soy sauce
2 1/2 tbsps sunflower oil
Fresh coriander leaves (chopped)

1. Place the garlic and coriander roots in a mortar and grind into a coarse paste with a pestle. Add the black peppercorns and grind in.

2. Heat the oil in a wok and add the paste. Stir-fry over a medium heat for 1-2 minutes, until fragrant.

3. Add the oyster sauce, soy sauce, vegetable stock and prawns and stir-fry for a further 2-3 minutes, until the prawns are cooked through and have turned pink.

Serve garnished with chopped coriander leaves.

Cucumber Salad (Serves 4)

1 large tomato (sliced)
4 spring onions (sliced)
2 small cucumbers (sliced)
1 onion (sliced in 1 inch lengths)
2 eggs
3-4 tbsps fish sauce
4 tbsps vinegar
4 tbsps vegetable oil
2 tbsps sugar

1. Place the vegetables in a bowl and combine together.

2. Place the 3 tablespoons of the fish sauce, vinegar, vegetable oil and sugar in a small bowl and whisk together. Taste and add more fish sauce, if desired. Add to the vegetables and toss together well.

Cucumber Salad/cont.

3. Fry the eggs, until the white is crispy and the yolk is cooked. Cut into bite-sized pieces.

4. Transfer the salad into a serving bowl and top with the egg pieces. Serve immediately.

Hot & Sour Soup with Pork & Broccoli (Serves 6)
750g/1 lb 11oz pork fillet (thinly sliced)
300g/2 cups of fresh Thai noodles
440g/2 1/2 cups of purple sprouting broccoli (cut into florets)
1 1/2 red onions (sliced)
7 kaffir lime leaves (finely shredded)
3 tsps Tom Yum paste
900ml/4 cups of boiling water
3 tbsps olive oil
1 handful parsley (chopped)

1. Heat the oil in a large saucepan over a medium heat and add the onion. Cook the onion slices and lime leaves for 3-4 minutes, until golden. Stir in the Tom Yum paste.

2. Add the water and bring the mixture to the boil. Add the broccoli, followed by the pork slices. Reduce the heat to a simmer and cook for 8-10 minutes.

3. Add the noodles and cook for a further 4-5 minutes, until the noodles are cooked.

4. Transfer to a large serving bowl and sprinkle chopped parsley over the top. Serve immediately.

Pork & Noodle Soup (Serves 4)
190g/2 1/2 cups of egg noodles (dried)
250g/9oz pork loin (cooked & cut into thin strips)
75g/3/4 cups of bean sprouts
2 litres chicken Thai soup stock
2 large lettuce leaves (shredded)

3 cloves of garlic (finely chopped)
2 tbsps fish sauce
1 tbsp sugar
1 tbsp vegetable oil
1-2 tbsps fresh coriander leaves (chopped)

1. Heat the vegetable oil in a frying pan and add the garlic. Fry for 2-4 minutes, until golden and crispy. Remove with a slotted spoon and set aside.

2. Pour the stock into a large saucepan and bring to the boil. Add the fish sauce, pork and sugar.

3. Reduce the heat and add the noodles; simmer for 4-5 minutes, until tender. Add the bean sprouts, shredded lettuce and garlic; stirring them in well.

4. Remove from the heat and pour into a large serving bowl. Garnish with fresh coriander leaves and serve immediately.

Prawn Parcels with Thai Chilli Sauce (Serves 6)

Prawn Parcels:
375g/13oz tiger prawns
6 sheets of frozen filo pastry (defrosted)
2-3 tbsps olive oil

Chilli Sauce:
4 Thai red chilli peppers (deseeded)
2 cloves of garlic (crushed)
450g/2 cups of canned, chopped tomatoes
1 shallot (minced)
75g/1/3 cup of sugar
75ml/1/3 cup of rice vinegar
1 tsp salt

Chilli Sauce:
1. Place all of the ingredients in a saucepan and bring to the boil. Reduce the heat, cover and simmer gently for 40-50 minutes, until thickened. Once thickened, transfer to a dish, for dipping.

Prawn Parcels with Thai Chilli Sauce/cont.

Prawn Parcels:

1. Preheat the oven to 240C/475F/Gas mark 9. Lightly grease a large baking tray.

2. Lay out one sheet of the filo pastry on a clean work surface and cut into 2cm strips, width-ways.

3. Brush each side of the strips with a little olive oil and wrap each strip around a tiger prawn, leaving the tail still visible.

4. Repeat this for the remaining sheets of pastry, until all of the prawns are wrapped. Transfer the prawns to the baking tray and place in the oven for 5-6 minutes, until golden.

5. Remove and serve hot with the chilli dipping sauce.

Prawn & Scallop Skewers (Serves 6)

450g/1 lb 1oz uncooked large prawns (shelled & deveined)
450g/1 lb 1oz scallops (removed from shells & trimmed)
1 large pineapple (cut into 1 inch cubes)
1 long red chilli (finely chopped)
3 cloves of garlic (finely chopped)
1 1/2 tbsps sesame oil
2 tbsps light soy sauce
1 tbsp coriander leaves (finely chopped)
1/2 tsp ground white pepper
Pre-soaked bamboo sticks

1. Place the chopped chilli, garlic, sesame oil, soy sauce, coriander leaves and white pepper in a bowl and mix together. Add the prawns and scallops and combine well. Cover and refrigerate for 1-2 hours.

2. Remove from the refrigerator 10 minutes before required. Thread the prawns and pineapple chunks, alternately, on half of the bamboo sticks and the scallops and remaining pineapple chunks on the other half.

3. Preheat the grill to a high temperature and grill the skewers for 18-20 minutes, turning halfway through cooking. Serve immediately.

Spicy Deep-Fried Fish Cakes (Makes approx. 12)

250g/9oz cod fillet (skinned)
15 green beans (finely chopped)
5 kaffir lime leaves (tightly rolled & cut into fine strips)
1 small egg (beaten)
1/2 tbsp fish sauce
1/2 tbsp palm sugar
3 tbsps red curry paste
2 tbsps tapioca starch
1 tsp baking powder
Vegetable oil (for deep frying)
Sweet chilli dip (for serving)

1. Place the fish in a food processor and blend until finely chopped. Add the finely cut kaffir lime leaves, fish sauce, palm sugar, baking powder, tapioca starch, red curry paste and beaten egg. Blend for 4-5 seconds, until roughly blended.

2. Transfer the mixture to a large bowl and stir in the chopped green beans. Cover and refrigerate for 8-12 hours.

Spicy Deep-Fried Fish Cakes/cont.

3. Heat 3-3 1/2 inches of vegetable oil in a wok to 170C/325F. Lightly dampen your hands to prevent sticking and separate the mixture into about 12 pieces; making small patties of about 2 inches in diameter.

4. Carefully add each fishcake to the hot oil and cook for 3-4 minutes, until golden brown and 'puffed-out' in size.

5. Carefully remove the fishcakes with a slotted spoon and drain off any excess fat on paper kitchen towel. Serve immediately with a green salad and sweet chilli dip.

Thai Barbeque Pork Ribs (Serves 8)

2kg pork spare ribs (cut into 5 inch lengths)
2 tbsps light soy sauce
5 cloves of garlic (finely chopped)
4 tbsps tomato ketchup
4 tbsps clear honey
1/2 tsp ground allspice
2 tsps ground coriander
1 tsp ground white pepper
2 red chillies (finely sliced)
2 spring onions (finely sliced)

1. Preheat the oven to 180C/350F/Gas mark 4.

2. Place the soy sauce, garlic, ketchup, clear honey, allspice, coriander and white pepper in a large bowl and combine. Add the pork ribs and using clean hands mix together, coating the pork ribs well.

3. Transfer the ribs and marinade into a large baking dish, (2 may be needed), and place in the oven for 50-60 minutes, basting regularly.

4. Remove from the oven and place under the grill on a high temperature. Cook for 5-6 minutes each side, until lightly charred.

5. Transfer the ribs to a large serving platter and garnish with chopped spring onions and chillies. Serve immediately.

Thai Curry Puffs (Makes 20)

700g/1 lb 9oz frozen puff pastry sheets (partially thawed)
220g/7 3/4oz cooked mashed potato
300g/1 1/3 cups of minced pork (lean)
1 clove of garlic (finely chopped)
1 onion (sliced)
2 tbsps chopped shallots
1 tbsp turmeric
1 tbsp sugar
4 tbsps vegetable oil
1 tbsp chopped coriander root
2 tsps salt
1 tsp black pepper
Vegetable oil (for deep frying)

1. Heat the vegetable oil in a wok, over a medium/high heat and add the garlic. Stir-fry for 2-3 minutes, until lightly browned. Add the coriander root, onion and turmeric and stir-fry for 3-4 minutes.

2. Add the minced meat, sugar, salt and pepper and stir-fry for 4-5 minutes, until the meat is heated through.

3. Reduce the heat a little and add the potato; stir-fry and mix all of the ingredients together well. Adjust the seasoning if required. Add the chopped shallots and stir-fry for 1 minute. Remove from the heat and transfer the mixture to a large bowl to cool.

4. Take one sheet of the puff pastry and cut into 4 equal-sized square pieces. Take one of the pieces and lay it with one of the flat corners towards you. Spoon 1 tablespoon of the cooled filling into the centre of the square and carefully lift the bottom corner and fold it over to the opposite corner; making a triangular parcel.

5. Seal the parcel with your fingers, pinching the pastry together along its edges. Make a twist in each wing of the pastry, firstly towards the centre and then away again. Place each of the parcels on a sheet of greaseproof paper. Repeat this process for the remaining mixture and pastry.

Thai Curry Puffs/cont.

6. Heat the vegetable oil in a wok and carefully drop in the parcels, cooking several at a time. Cook for 3-4 minutes, until golden brown.

7. Carefully remove with a slotted spoon and drain off any excess fat on paper kitchen towel.

Serve hot with relishes or satay sauce.

Thai Tiger Prawn & Vegetable Platter (Serves 6)

400g/14oz cooked tiger prawns (peeled, tails left on)
225g/2 1/4 cups of fresh bean sprouts
150g/5oz baby carrots (thinly sliced, lengthways)
150g/5oz baby corn (thinly sliced, lengthways)
150g/5oz sugar snap peas (halved, lengthways)
Large bunch of spring onions (thinly sliced, diagonally)
Large bunch of radishes (thinly sliced)
2 lettuces (web or iceberg)
2 cloves of garlic (finely chopped)
50g/1/3 cup of roasted peanuts (chopped)
Zest & juice of 3 limes
6 tsps sugar
3 tsps fish sauce
3 tbsps vegetable oil
Salt (to season)

1. Place the vegetable oil, garlic, sugar, fish sauce, lime zest and juice in a bowl. Place the prawns in a large bowl and add one third of the mixed dressing. Toss gently to coat the prawns. Set aside.

2. Place the bean sprouts, baby corn, sugar snap peas, baby carrots, radishes and spring onions in a pan and gently combine together. Add to the prawns and pour in the remaining dressing. Add a pinch of salt and gently toss the ingredients together.

3. Lay the lettuce leaves out on a large serving platter and spoon the prawn salad over the top. Sprinkle with chopped peanuts and serve.

Salads
&
Snacks

Beef Salad (Serves 8)

500g/1 lb 2oz cooked roast beef (preferably still a little pink in the middle & cut into thin strips)
125g/1 1/4 cup of celery (chopped)
35 fresh small green & red chillies (chopped)
2 cucumbers (halved, lengthways; deseeded & chopped into half-moons)
2 large tomatoes (cored & cut into thick wedges)
6 tbsps sliced French shallots
8-10 spring onions (cut into 1 inch pieces)
150ml/2/3 cup of fish sauce
170ml/3/4 cup of fresh lime juice
2 tsps palm sugar
2 tbsps vegetable oil

1. Place the lime juice, fish sauce, sugar and chillies in a bowl and combine together until the sugar has dissolved.

2. Add the meat strips to the fish sauce mixture and toss together. Add the shallots, tomatoes, cucumber, spring onions and celery and toss gently to coat all the ingredients.

Transfer to a large serving dish and serve immediately.

Crispy Fried Calamari (Serves 4)

325g/11 1/2oz calamari rings (rinsed, drained & dried)
112g/1 1/4 cup of dried breadcrumbs
1 egg (lightly beaten)
1 tsp sugar
1/2 tsp salt
1/2 tsp pepper
Vegetable oil (for deep frying)

1. Place the egg, sugar, salt and pepper in a bowl and mix together. Add the calamari to the bowl and leave to marinate for 10-15 minutes.

2. Remove the calamari from the bowl and drain in a colander for 15 minutes. Place the breadcrumbs on a plate and lightly roll in the calamari.

Crispy Fried Calamari/cont.

3. Heat the vegetable oil in a wok and carefully add the calamari, several at a time. Cook for a few minutes at a time, until golden brown.

4. Remove with a slotted spoon and drain off any excess fat on paper kitchen towel. Serve immediately with sweet chilli sauce.

Cherry Tomato & Spring Onion Omelette (Serves 4-6)

6 large eggs
12 cherry tomatoes (halved)
6 spring onions (finely chopped)
2 tbsps vegetable oil
1 1/2 tbsps light soy sauce
Ground white pepper (to season)
Fresh coriander leaves (optional)

1. Place the eggs, white pepper and soy sauce in a bowl and whisk together, until frothed-up. Add the cherry tomatoes and spring onions and mix together.

2 Heat the vegetable oil in a wok and add the egg mixture. Cook over a medium heat for 2-3 minutes, until the underneath is lightly brown.

3. Carefully flip the omelette over to cook the other side for another 2-3 minutes, until lightly browned.

4. Transfer to a serving dish and garnish with coriander leaves, if desired. Slice into the required amount of slices and serve.

Crispy Stir-Fried Vegetables (Serves 4)

12 baby sweetcorn (halved, lengthways)
135g/3/4 cup of green beans (halved, lengthways)
135g/3/4 cup of red & yellow peppers (deseeded & cut into pieces)
12 thin asparagus spears (tips cut off, but retained & stalks cut into 2 inch lengths)
135g/3/4 cup of mange tout (trimmed)
135g/3/4 cup of broccoli florets

125g/1 1/4 cup of bean sprouts
150g/1 cup of small courgettes (thinly sliced)
1 medium carrot (peeled & cut into strips)
1 tbsp sesame seeds
3 cloves of garlic (finely chopped)
1 inch fresh root ginger (peeled & finely sliced)
4 tbsps vegetable stock
1 1/2 tbsps sunflower oil
2 tbsps oyster sauce
1 tbsp light soy sauce

1. Dry-fry the sesame seeds in a saucepan for 1-2 minutes, until golden. Remove from the pan and set aside.

2. Blanch the sweetcorn, green beans, broccoli florets, asparagus stalks, mange tout, carrot and courgettes in boiling water for 30-40 seconds. Remove immediately and transfer to a bowl of cold water, to retain the vegetables' crispy texture.

3. Drain the blanched vegetables thoroughly and place them in a large bowl. Add the peppers, bean sprouts, asparagus tips and sliced ginger. Carefully toss the ingredients together.

4. Heat the oil in a wok and add the garlic. Stir-fry over a medium heat until golden. Add the vegetables, oyster sauce, light soy sauce and vegetable stock and stir-fry over a high heat for 3-4 minutes.

5. Remove from the heat and transfer to a serving dish. Serve immediately.

Curried Bamboo Shoots & Minced Pork (Serves 6)
325g/11 1/2oz canned shredded bamboo shoots (drained)
225g/1 cup of minced pork
1 1/2-2 tbsps Thai red curry paste
1 1/2 tbsps vegetable oil
1 tbsp fish sauce

1. Heat the vegetable oil in a wok and add the red curry paste. Stir-fry for 2-3 minutes, until fragrant.

Curried Bamboo Shoots & Minced Pork/cont.

2. Add the minced pork and stir-fry for 5-6 minutes, until the pork has cooked through.

3. Stir in the fish sauce and bamboo shoots and stir-fry for a further 2-3 minutes. Remove from the heat and transfer to a serving dish.

Green Bean & Papaya Salad (Serves 4)
8-10 green beans (cut into 1 inch pieces)
500g/1 lb 2oz green papaya (peeled, seeded & cut into long, thin strips)
6 cherry tomatoes (halved)
8-10 small fresh green chillies
2 large cloves of garlic (peeled)
2 tbsps dried shrimp
1 tsp palm sugar
2 tbsps fish sauce
2 tbsps fresh lime juice
2 tbsps roasted peanuts (coarsely ground)

1. Place the chillies, green beans and garlic in a large mortar and pound with a pestle, to bruise the ingredients not grind them. Add the green papaya strips to the mortar and bruise with the pestle again.

2. Add the fish sauce, palm sugar, lime juice and dried shrimp and stir together until the sugar has dissolved.

3. Stir in the tomatoes. Combine all of the ingredients together well.

4. Transfer to a serving dish and sprinkle with coarsely ground peanuts. Serve immediately.

Mixed Mushrooms with Ginger (Serves 4)
600g/1 lb 5oz mushrooms; button, shitake, oyster, chestnut, etc (large ones halved and hard stalks removed)
1 onion (cut into wedges)
1 tsp dried black fungus (soaked for 2 minutes & drained)
4 cloves of garlic (finely chopped)
2 tbsps oyster sauce

2 inches of fresh root ginger (peeled & finely sliced)
2 spring onions (slivered)
2 tbsps sunflower oil
4 tbsps vegetable stock

1. Remove the hard stalks from the dried black fungus and discard. Heat the oil in a wok and add the garlic. Stir-fry over a medium heat for 2-3 minutes, until golden brown.

2. Add the mushrooms to the wok, followed by the onion, black fungus, ginger, spring onions, oyster sauce and vegetable stock. Stir-fry over a high heat for 5 minutes.

Transfer to a serving dish and serve immediately.

Prawn Salad (Serves 6)
Salad:
675g/1 1/2 lbs uncooked large prawns (shelled & deveined)
3 cloves of garlic (finely sliced)
4 kaffir lime leaves (finely sliced)
1 1/2 bags of mixed salad leaves
3 lemon grass stalks (white only, finely sliced)

Dressing:
2-3 small red chillies (finely chopped)
1 1/2 tbsps fish sauce
10 tbsps lime juice

1. Place the dressing ingredients in a bowl and mix together.

2. Cook the prawns in boiling water for 2-3 minutes. Drain thoroughly and leave to cool.

3. Place the garlic, kaffir lime leaves, lemon grass, salad dressing and cooled prawns in a large bowl and toss together. Place mixed salad leaves on each serving plate and top with the prawn salad.

Serve immediately.

Salads & Snacks

Spiced Chilli Burgers – Thai-Style (Serves 6)

750g/3 & 1/3 cups of minced beef
1-2 red chillies (chopped)
3 cloves of garlic (chopped)
10 spring onions (chopped)
Zest & juice of 1 1/2 limes
150g/1 cup of salted peanuts
Bunch of fresh coriander (chopped)
1/2 cucumber (sliced)
Salt & black pepper (to season)
Sweet chilli sauce (to serve)

1. Place the chillies, garlic, spring onions and peanuts in a food processor and process, until finely chopped. Transfer to a large bowl.

2. Add the minced beef, lime zest and juice and the chopped coriander to the bowl and season with salt and black pepper. Combine all of the ingredients together well.

3. Using dampened hands, shape the mixture into balls and flatten lightly using the palm of your hands into a burger shapes. Place on a plate, cover and refrigerate for 1 hour.

4. Preheat the grill to a medium temperature and place the burgers on a grill pan. Place under the grill for 3-4 minutes, each side.

5. Serve the burgers in toasted baps, with a slice of cucumber and with a little sweet chilli sauce.

Salty Beef Strips (Serves 6)

1.5kg/3 lbs 5oz beef steak fillets
7 tbsps coarse salt
Vegetable oil (for deep frying)

1. Rub the steak fillets with salt and lay on top of each in other in a dish. Cover and refrigerate overnight.

2. Remove from the refrigerator and drain off any liquids. Heat the oil in a frying pan and add the steaks. Cook over a high heat so that the steaks become crispy and golden on the outside.

3. Remove and set aside to cool a little. Once cooled enough, slice into 1 inch thick slices. Serve warm with a side salad, or as an accompaniment to a Thai curry dish.

Spicy Pork Balls in Lettuce Leaves (serves 4-6)

450g/2 cups of minced pork
6 iceberg lettuce leaves (washed & patted dry)
2 red chillies (finely sliced)
2 tbsps chilli sauce
2 tbsps fish sauce
1/2 stalk of lemon grass
1 handful of mint (chopped)
1 handful of Thai basil (chopped)
1 small handful of coriander (with roots, chopped)
1/4 tsp black pepper
Groundnut oil (for frying)

1. Place the fresh chillies, lemon grass, mint, Thai basil, coriander and black pepper in a spice grinder and blend together. Alternatively use a mortar and pestle to grind the ingredients together.

2. Place the pork mince in a bowl and sprinkle in the ground herbs and spices. Combine together well. Using wet hands, shape the mixture into small meatballs.

Salads & Snacks

Spicy Pork Balls in Lettuce Leaves/cont.

3. Place the chilli sauce and fish sauce in a bowl and mix together well. Set aside.

4. Heat a couple of inches of the oil in a frying pan and carefully add the meatballs. Cook for 5-6 minutes, until the meatballs are cooked through.

5. Remove with a slotted spoon and drain off any excess fat on paper kitchen towel.

6. Wrap the pork balls in the lettuce leaves and drizzle over the top with the fish and chilli sauce.

Serve immediately.

Thai-Style Green Salad (Serves 4-6)
1 large head of Cos lettuce (shredded)
1 bunch of spring onions (sliced diagonally)
3/4 cucumber
2 tbsps Thai fish sauce
4 tbsps fresh lime juice
1 tsp sugar
1 fresh, red chilli (finely chopped)
1 clove of garlic (crushed)
1 tbsp fresh mint (chopped)
2 tbsps fresh coriander (chopped)
2 tbsps toasted fresh coconut (shredded)

1. Place the lettuce and spring onions in a large salad bowl.

2. Using a vegetable peeler, slice the cucumber lengthways, creating thin shavings. Add to the salad bowl. Place the remaining ingredients in a mixing jug and whisk together well.

3. Pour the dressing over the salad and toss gently, coating all the leaves.

4. Sprinkle over the top with the coconut and toss again. Serve immediately, or cover and refrigerate until ready to serve.

Main Dishes

Aromatic Thai Salmon with Pak Choy (Serves 6)

6 salmon fillets (approx. 180g/6 1/2oz)
675g/9 cups of pak choy
4 cloves of garlic (crushed)
1 clove of garlic (finely sliced)
18 mint leaves (washed)
125g/5oz spring onions (finely sliced)
3 green chillies (deseeded)
3 red chillies (deseeded & finely chopped)
4 1/2 tbsps fresh lime juice
3 tsps chopped fresh ginger
1 1/2 tbsps fish sauce
1 1/2 tbsps soy sauce
3 tbsps caster sugar
1 1/2 tbsps vegetable oil
1 1/2 tbsps sesame oil
1 large bunch of fresh coriander (washed)
1 1/2 tsps salt
Salt & black pepper (to season)

1. Place the mint, coriander, green chillies, crushed garlic and salt in a food processor and blend into a paste.

2. Add one tablespoon of the caster sugar, fish sauce, lime juice and one teaspoon of chopped ginger and process again, until smooth. Transfer into a bowl and add the salmon.

3. Using clean hands, cover the salmon with the marinade and set aside to marinate for 20-30 minutes.

4. Boil some water in the bottom part of a steamer and place the salmon/marinade bowl in the top part of the steamer. Steam for 7-8 minutes.

NB. If this has to be completed in two batches, keep the first batch warm, but be careful not to dry it out.

Main Dishes

Aromatic Thai Salmon with Pak Choy/cont.

5. Boil some salted water in a saucepan and add the pak choy. Cook for 2 minutes, drain and immediately run under cold water. Drain again and set aside.

6. Heat the vegetable and sesame oil in a wok and add the spring onions, red chillies, remaining ginger and sliced garlic. Stir-fry for 1-2 minutes.

7. Stir in the remaining caster sugar, pak choy and soy sauce. Cook, tossing continuously, for 1-2 minutes. Season with salt and black pepper, according to taste. Remove from the heat.

8. Equally divide the pak choy mixture between serving plates and top with the salmon fillets.

Beef with Peppers (Serves 6)
450g/1 lb fillet steak (thinly sliced)
1 large onion (sliced)
3 spring onions (finely sliced)
220g/1 1/4 cups of red & green peppers (deseeded & cut into chunks)
4 cloves of garlic (finely chopped)
2 1/2 tbsps vegetable oil
5 1/2 tbsps beef stock
1 tbsp oyster sauce
Ground white pepper

1. Heat the oil in a wok and add the garlic. Stir-fry the garlic over a medium heat for 2-3 minutes, until lightly browned.

2. Add the beef strips to the wok and stir-fry for 3-4 minutes. Add the onion, red and green peppers, beef stock and oyster sauce, and stir-fry for a further 2-3 minutes.

3. Add the chopped spring onions, stirring them in. Transfer to a serving dish and season with white pepper, according to taste.

Serve immediately with hot boiled rice, or hot noodles.

Beef Steak with Hot-Shallot Sauce (Serves 4)

900g - 1.2kg/2 – 2 1/2 lbs sirloin/rump or fillet steak
4 shallots (thinly sliced)
2 tsps ground dried chillies
Juice of 1 1/2 limes
4-6 tbsps fish sauce
2 tsps toasted rice (crushed)

1. Grill the steaks, according to personal requirements, (i.e. rare, medium, well done, etc).

2. Whilst the steaks are cooking, grind the toasted rice in a spice grinder, or with a mortar and pestle.

3. Place the fish sauce, toasted rice, lime juice, sliced shallots and chillies in a bowl and combine well. Taste and add more fish sauce, if desired.

4. Once cooked, slice the steaks into 1 inch strips and serve over rice, with the hot-shallot sauce.

Chicken & Cashew Nuts (Serves 4)

550g/1 lb 4oz chicken breast (skinless & finely sliced)
115g/3/4 cup of dry-fried cashew nuts
3 cloves of garlic (finely chopped)
1/2 red pepper (deseeded & chopped)
1 carrot (cut into thin strips)
3 spring onions (finely sliced)
1 onion (quartered)
1 1/2 tbsps oyster sauce
1 tbsp light soy sauce
2 dried, long red chillies (deseeded & cut into 1/2 inch pieces)
2 tbsps sunflower oil
3 tbsps chicken stock
Ground white pepper (to season)

1. Heat 1 tablespoon of oil in a wok and add the chopped chillies. Stir-fry over a medium heat for 1-2 minutes. Remove with a slotted spoon and set aside.

Chicken & Cashew Nuts/cont.

2. Add 1 tablespoon of oil to the wok and add the garlic. Stir-fry for 1-2 minutes, until golden brown. Add the chicken pieces and stock and stir-fry over a high heat for 5-6 minutes, until cooked through.

3. Add the carrot, red pepper, oyster sauce, onion and soy sauce and stir-fry for 2-3 minutes. Add the chillies, cashew nuts and spring onions and stir-fry for 30 seconds.

4. Remove from the heat and transfer to a serving dish. Season with white pepper, according to taste.

Serve immediately with hot rice.

Chicken Legs with Garlic & Lemon Grass (Serves 6)

12 chicken legs
10 cloves of garlic (peeled)
4 stalks of lemon grass (white part, peeled & chopped)
3 spring onions (finely chopped)
3 tbsps dry white wine
3 tbsps fresh lime juice
3 tbsps fish sauce
160ml/2/3 cup of coconut milk
1 1/2 tbsps toasted sesame oil
1/2 tsps black pepper (to season)

1. Place the lemon grass and garlic in a large mortar and pound together with a pestle, into a coarse paste.

2. Add the chopped spring onions, white wine, lime juice, fish sauce, coconut milk, sesame oil and black pepper and stir all of the ingredients together well.

3. Arrange the chicken legs in a shallow dish and pour the marinade evenly over the top. Shake the chicken in the dish to coat more evenly. Cover and refrigerate for 4-8 hours; turning the chicken over 2-3 times.

4. Remove from the refrigerator and stand at room temperature for 20-30 minutes before cooking.

5. Preheat the grill to a medium/high heat and lay the chicken legs on a grill pan. Cook about 8-10 inches from the flame for 20-25 minutes, turning occasionally, until the chicken is cooked through and golden.

Serve immediately.

Fried Snapper with Thai Basil & Chilli Dressing (Serves 6)

2-3 red snappers (8-9 inches long – scaled, gutted & each scored 3 times to the bone with a sharp knife)
110ml/1/2 cup of chicken stock
25g/1oz sweet Thai basil leaves (chopped)
7 fresh medium red chillies (thinly sliced)
1 fresh long red chilli (cut into large pieces)
1 fresh long green chilli (cut into large pieces)
7 cloves of garlic (chopped)
1 large onion (finely chopped)
1 1/2 tbsps fish sauce
1 1/2 tbsps soy sauce
25g/1oz fresh coriander leaves (chopped)
6-8 tbsps vegetable oil

1. Heat 4-5 tbsps of vegetable oil in a large wok to 180C/350F. Carefully add each fish and cook for 8-12 minutes, until browned and crispy on both sides, (variable cooking time will depend on size).

2. Remove each fish carefully and drain off any excess fat on paper kitchen towel. Retain in a large dish.

3. Heat 2-3 tablespoons of vegetable oil in a separate wok and add the onion, garlic and all the chopped chillies. Stir-fry for 3-4 minutes, until the garlic is lightly browned.

4. Add the soy sauce, chicken stock and fish sauce and stir together well. Cook for 1-2 minutes. Remove from the heat. Add the sweet Thai basil leaves and stir in well. Pour the mixture over the fish.

5. Transfer the fish to a large serving platter and sprinkle evenly over the top with chopped coriander leaves. Serve immediately.

Lemon Grass Pork Stir-Fry (Serves 4)

550g/1 lb 5oz boneless pork loin (cut crossways into 1/4-inch thick slices, then cut into 1/4-inch strips)
2 lemon grass stalks (finely chopped)
2 fresh red chillies (seeded & chopped)
4 spring onions (finely sliced)
2 cloves of garlic (finely chopped)
2 tbsps roasted unsalted peanuts (chopped)
2 tbsps fish sauce
10-12 black peppercorns (coarsely crushed)
1 tsp soft light brown sugar
1 tbsp vegetable oil
1 tsp salt
Black pepper (to season)
2 tbsps fresh coriander leaves (shredded)
Cooked rice noodles (to serve)

1. Place the pork in a bowl and add the spring onions, lemon grass, peppercorns and salt, and combine well. Cover and refrigerate for 30-40 minutes.

2. Preheat a wok and add the vegetable oil, covering the wok well. Add the pork mixture and stir-fry over a medium heat for 4 minutes, until browned.

3. Add the red chillies and garlic and stir-fry for 6-8 minutes, over a medium heat, until tender. Stir in the fish sauce, chopped peanuts and sugar, tossing all the ingredients together. Season with salt and black pepper, according to taste.

4. Serve immediately over rice noodles and garnish with shredded coriander leaves.

Lime & Coriander Chicken (Serves 6)
6 chicken breasts (skinless)
6 cloves of garlic (finely chopped)
3 tsps Thai fish sauce
Juice of 3 limes
3 tsps black peppercorns (coarsely ground)
3 tsps caster sauce
1 1/2 tbsps light soy sauce
2 tbsps vegetable oil
4 tbsps fresh coriander leaves (finely chopped)

1. Place the peppercorns, garlic, coriander, fish sauce, vegetable oil, soy sauce and lime juice in a large bowl and combine well.

2. Add the chicken breasts to the bowl and cover well with the marinade. Cover and refrigerate for 2 hours, turning occasionally.

3. Preheat a non-stick frying pan over a medium heat and add the marinated chicken.

4. Cook for 8-9 minutes on each side, until cooked through and golden.

Serve with rice, and/or vegetables.

Piquant Ground Beef with Basil (Serves 4)

600g/1 lb 5oz minced beef
250ml/1 & 1/8 cup of chicken stock
12 cloves of garlic (crushed)
2 fresh long red chillies (cut into large pieces)
8-10 fresh red & green chillies (coarsely chopped)
2 tbsps fish sauce
1 tbsp oyster sauce
3 tbsps vegetable oil
1 tbsp sugar
1 tsp sweet soy sauce
50g/1/2 cup fresh basil leaves

1. Heat the vegetable oil in a large wok over a high heat and add the smaller chillies and garlic. Stir-fry for 3 minutes, until the garlic browns a little.

2. Add the minced beef and stir-fry for 2-3 minutes, until lightly browned. Stir in the fish sauce, oyster sauce, sugar and soy sauce, and combine well.

3. Add the larger chopped chillies and chicken stock and bring to the boil. Reduce the heat a little and simmer for 1 minute. Add the basil and cook for a further minute.

4. Remove from the heat and transfer to a serving dish. Serve piping hot.

Prawn Stir-Fry (Serves 4-6)

400g/14oz cooked peeled prawns
5 spring onions (halved lengthways & cut into 4cm strips)
1/2 cucumber (cut into thin 4cm strips)
150g/1 1/2 cups of mushrooms (sliced)
1/2 tsp Thai fish sauce
1 tsp red chilli (deseeded & chopped)
1 tsp fresh root ginger (grated)
1 clove of garlic (crushed)
1 tbsp dark soy sauce
2 tbsps dry sherry
2 tbsps vegetable oil
2 tsps cornflour

1. Heat the oil in a preheated wok and add the cucumber, spring onions, mushrooms, garlic, chilli and ginger. Stir-fry for 2-3 minutes.

2. Add the prawns to the wok and stir-fry for 1 minute. Place the soy sauce, water, cornflour and fish sauce in a mixing jug and mix together, until smooth. Stir into the wok.

3. Pour in the dry sherry and continue to cook, until the sauce thickens. Serve immediately.

Sea Bass in Chilli Sauce (Serves 4)
1 whole sea bass, approx. 675g/1 lb 10oz (scaled, cleaned & gutted)
3 tbsps plain flour
65ml of dry white wine
1 red jalapeno pepper (thinly sliced)
1 green jalapeno pepper (thinly sliced)
4 cloves of garlic (finely sliced)
40g/1/4 cup of onion (thinly sliced)
55ml/1/4 cup of fish sauce
1 tbsp fresh basil (chopped)
3 tbsps fresh coriander (chopped)
2 tbsps vegetable oil
Vegetable oil (for deep frying)

1. Preheat the oven to 180C/350F/Gas mark 4. Make three deep diagonal cuts on both sides of the fish and sprinkle over with white wine.

2. Lay the flour out on a large plate and coat the fish on both sides. Place the fish in a pan of hot oil and deep fry for 1-2 minutes.

3. Carefully remove from the pan and transfer to a shallow ovenproof dish. Place in the oven for 20-25 minutes, until cooked through.

4. Whilst the fish is cooking, heat the 2 tablespoons of vegetable oil in a wok and add the onions and chillies. Stir-fry for 3-4 minutes, until the onions are lightly golden.

Sea Bass in Chilli Sauce/cont.

5. Stir in the fish sauce and bring to a simmer. Add the chopped coriander leaves and cook, stirring continuously for 4-5 minutes, until the fish sauce has reduced a little. Remove from the heat and leave to cool.

6. Once the sauce has cooled, stir in the basil leaves and transfer to a pouring jug.

7. Once the fish is ready, place on a warmed serving platter and serve with the sauce.

Spiced Chicken Livers (Serves 6)

450g/1 lb chicken livers (washed, dried & cut into 1 1/2 inch pieces)
4 shallots (cut into 1 inch pieces)
9 dried Chinese mushrooms (soaked for 20 minutes in hot water & drained)
2 large onions (sliced)
2 cloves of garlic (finely chopped)
3 fresh red chillies (finely sliced)
2 tbsps fish sauce
2 tbsps lemon juice
1/4 green pepper (deseeded & sliced)
3 tbsps vegetable oil
1 tsp sugar

1. Remove the stems from the mushrooms and finely slice them. Set aside.

2. Heat the oil in a wok and add the garlic. Stir-fry for 2-3 minutes, until golden brown. Add the chillies and onion and stir-fry for 1-2 minutes.

3. Add the chicken livers and stir-fry until just turned pink. Add the lemon juice, mushrooms, fish sauce and sugar and stir-fry for 1-2 minutes.

4. Taste and adjust seasonings if desired. Add the green pepper and shallots and stir-fry for a further 1-2 minutes.

Remove from the heat and serve immediately with hot rice.

Stir-Fried Lamb with Mint & Chilli (Serves 4)

225g/8 oz lean lamb (cut into thin strips)
1 tbsp fish sauce
1 tbsp oyster sauce
1 clove of garlic (finely sliced)
1-2 fresh chillies (finely sliced)
3 tbsps vegetable oil
4 tbsps fresh mint leaves (sliced)
Pinch of sugar

1. Heat the vegetable oil in a
wok and add the lamb strips.
Stir-fry the lamb for 4-5 minutes,
until almost cooked.

2. Add the garlic, fish sauce, oyster sauce, chilli and sugar. Stir-fry for a
further 1-2 minutes. Adjust the seasonings if desired.

3. Once the meat is tender, add the mint leaves, stirring them in well.
Remove from the heat. Serve immediately with hot boiled rice.

Stir-Fried Mussels with Garlic & Chilli (Serves 6)

750g/1 lb 11oz mussels (scrubbed clean)
225ml/1 cup of chicken stock
3 cloves of garlic (chopped)
4 fresh chillies (chopped)
1 1/2 tbsps fish sauce
2 1/2 tbsps oyster sauce
1 1/2 tbsps chopped coriander root
4 tbsps vegetable oil
4 tbsps chopped, fresh basil leaves

1. Place the chillies, coriander root and garlic in a spice grinder and process
into a rough paste, (alternatively use a mortar and pestle).

2. Heat the oil in a wok and add the paste, stir-fry for 1-2 minutes until
blended and fragrant. Add the oyster and fish sauces, stirring them in well.

Stir-Fried Mussels with Garlic & Chilli/cont.

3. Pour in the chicken stock and add the mussels. Bring just to the boil and then reduce the heat. Cover and simmer for 10 minutes, until the mussels open and are cooked.

4. Taste the sauce and adjust the seasoning, if desired.

5. Stir in the basil and remove from the heat. Transfer to a large serving dish and serve hot with hot boiled rice, or a side salad.

Rice
&
Noodles

Chicken & Vegetable Noodles with Ginger (Serves 4)

525g/1 lb 3oz chicken breast (skinless & sliced)
450g/3 cups of Thai ribbon noodles
115ml/1/2 cup of chicken stock
2 cloves of garlic (finely chopped)
125g/5oz baby corn (halved, lengthways)
150g/1 cup of sugarsnap peas
175g/1 cup of broccoli florets
2 carrots (cut into thin batons)
1 red pepper (deseeded & sliced)
1 inch fresh root ginger (finely chopped)
2-3 tbsps sweet chilli sauce
2 tbsps fresh coriander (chopped)
2 tbsps vegetable oil

1. Cook the noodles, as per the packet instructions. Drain thoroughly and set aside.

2. Heat the oil in a wok and add the chicken strips. Stir-fry for 8-10 minutes. Add the peppers, broccoli and carrots and stir-fry for 4-5 minutes. Add the sugar snap peas, baby corn, garlic and ginger and stir-fry for 3-4 minutes.

3. Stir in the chicken stock, noodles, coriander and chilli sauce and combine. Stir-fry for 1 minute. Remove from the heat and transfer to a serving dish.

Citrus Brown Rice (Serves 4-6)
375g/1 & 2/3 cup of easy-cook brown rice (rinsed)
2 limes (rind pared & set aside)
1 stalk of lemon grass (finely chopped)
1 onion (chopped)
840ml/3 3/4 cups of hot vegetable stock
2 tsp coriander seeds
2 tsps cumin seeds
1 inch piece of fresh root ginger (finely chopped)
3 tbsps chopped fresh coriander leaves
1-2 tbsps vegetable oil
Salt & black pepper (to season)
Spring onions (finely chopped – to garnish)

To be cooked in a slow cooker.

1. Heat the vegetable oil in a large saucepan and add the onion. Cook for 4-5 minutes, until tender. Add the cumin seeds, coriander seeds and ginger, stirring them in well. Cook for 2-3 minutes.

2. Transfer the mixture into the slow cooker's ceramic pot. Add the hot stock to the pot and stir. Cover and cook for 1 hour on a high setting.

3. Add the rice to the slow cooker and re-cover. Cook 1-1 1/2 hours, until the rice is cooked and the stock has been absorbed. Turn off the heat.

4. Stir in the chopped coriander and season with salt and black pepper, according to taste. Fluff the rice and transfer to a serving dish. Garnish with spring onions and serve immediately.

Coconut Rice (Serves 6-8)
525g/2 & 1/3 cups of basmati rice
1 inch piece of fresh ginger (finely sliced)
50g/2oz creamed coconut (chopped)
1 bay leaf
1 cinnamon stick
3 cloves

1 tsp salt
1 stalk of lemon grass (halved)
3 strips of lime rind
2 1/2 tsps ground nutmeg
1.2 ltrs of water
Black pepper (to season)

1. Place the water in large saucepan and add the lemon grass, nutmeg, creamed coconut, cinnamon, bay leaf, lime rind, salt, cloves and ginger. Slowly bring the mixture to the boil.

2. Add the rice, stirring the ingredients in together. Reduce the heat, cover and simmer gently for 20-30 minutes, (dependant on package instructions) – until all the water has been absorbed and the rice is cooked.

3. Remove from the heat and season with black pepper, according to taste. Fluff the rice with a fork and remove the lemon rind, bay leaf, cloves and cinnamon stick. Serve whilst still piping hot.

Crab Risotto (Serves 6)
700g/1 lb 9oz fresh white & dark crab meat
450ml/2 cups of hot chicken stock
450ml/2 cups of hot fish stock
450g/2 cups of Arborio rice
150ml/2/3 cup of dry white wine
80ml/1/3 cup of double cream
2 tbsps Thai green curry paste (according to taste)
3 shallots (finely chopped)
3 cloves of garlic (finely chopped)
125g/1 cup of Parmesan cheese (grated)
3 tbsps Mascarpone cheese
3 kaffir lime leaves
2-3 green chillies (finely chopped)
1 stick of lemon grass (crushed)
Juice of 1 1/2 limes
3 tbsps butter
2 tsps flat leaf parsley (chopped)

Crab Risotto/cont.

2 tbsps fresh coriander (chopped)
Black pepper (to season)
Extra Parmesan (to garnish)

1. Melt the butter in a large, deep frying pan and add the shallots and garlic. Stir-fry for 1-2 minutes.

2. Pour in the wine and add the rice. Stir in the curry paste, lemon grass, kaffir lime leaves and green chillies.

3. Place the chicken stock and fish stock in a large mixing jug and stir together. Using a ladle, spoon some of the mixed stock into the frying pan and cook, stirring, until the rice has absorbed the liquid. Continue this process until all the stock has been absorbed.

4. Remove and discard the lemon grass and stir in the coriander, parsley and Mascarpone.

5. Add the crabmeat and Parmesan cheese, followed by the lime juice and cream. Season with black pepper, according to taste.

Transfer to a warmed serving dish and garnish with Parmesan.

Easy Noodle Salad (Serves 4)

600g/1 lb 5oz dried egg noodles
10-12 small bulbs of pak choy (leaves separated)
4 cloves of garlic (finely chopped)
3-4 red chillies (finely chopped)
2 inches fresh root ginger (peeled & grated)
6 tbsps soy sauce
2 tbsps sesame oil
Juice of 2 limes
3 tbsps vegetable oil
Wedges of lime (to garnish)

1. Cook the egg noodles as per the packet instructions. Heat the vegetable oil in a large wok and add the ginger, chilli and garlic. Stir-fry for 1-2 minutes.

2. Add the pak choy leaves and stir-fry for 1-2 minutes, until starting to wilt. Add the lime juice, sesame oil and soy sauce and bring to a simmer for 1-2 minutes.

3. Add the freshly cooked noodles and toss all of the ingredients together. Remove from the heat and transfer to a large serving dish.

Serve immediately with lime wedges.

Fried Rice with Pineapple (Serves 4)

480g/2 & 1/8 cups of cooked long-grain jasmine rice
100g/1/2 cup of fresh pineapple (chopped)
1 large tomato (chopped)
3 spring onions (chopped)
1 onion (chopped)
100g/2/3 cup of sultanas
2 Chinese sausages (cut into small pieces)
2 tbsps butter
2 tbsps soy sauce
55ml/1/4 cup of vegetable oil
1/2 tsp curry powder
1 tsp sugar

Fried Rice with Pineapple/cont.

1. Heat the vegetable oil in a wok and add the chopped sausages. Cook for 1-2 minutes. Remove with a slotted spoon and drain on paper kitchen towel.

2. Add the butter and curry powder to the wok and fry, stirring continuously, for 1 minute. Stir in the cooked rice, coating it in the butter well.

3. Add the chopped onion, spring onions, sausages, sultanas, pineapple and tomato. Stir-fry for 4-5 minutes.

4. Stir in the soy sauce and sugar and cook for a further minute. Remove from the heat and serve immediately.

Fried Rice Noodles with Prawns (Serves 6)

375g/13oz rice noodles
18 uncooked king prawns (shelled – tails intact & deveined)
250g/2 1/2 bean sprouts
50g/1/3 cup of roasted peanuts (roughly ground)
120g/4 1/4oz garlic chives (cut into 2 inch lengths)
4 tbsps fried bean curd (cut into slivers)
2 cloves of garlic (finely chopped)
2 eggs (lightly beaten)
2 tbsp fish sauce
2 tbsp pickled white radish
2 tbsp tamarind juice
1 tbsp dark soy sauce
3 tbsp vegetable oil
1 tsp sugar
1 tsp dried chilli flakes
2 tbsp coriander leaves (to garnish)

1. Soak the noodles in warm water for 20-25 minutes and then drain thoroughly.

2. Heat one tablespoon of vegetable oil in a wok and add the garlic. Cook for 3-4 minutes, until golden brown. Add the prawns and cook for 2 minutes, until pink – tossing occasionally. Remove from the wok with a slotted spoon and set aside.

3. Heat another tablespoon of vegetable oil in the wok and add the eggs. Move the wok around, spreading the eggs around the insides to make a thin sheet. Stir the eggs to scramble then remove from the wok. Set aside.

4. Heat the remaining vegetable oil in the wok and add the bean curd, dried chillies and pickled radish. Cook, stirring continuously, for 1 minute. Add the drained noodles and stir-fry for 4-5 minutes.

5. Add half the bean sprouts, half the ground peanuts and the garlic chives. Stir in the fish sauce, tamarind juice, soy sauce and sugar. Mix together well and cook until the noodles are heated through.

6. Return the eggs and prawns to the wok and combine well. Cook for 1-2 minutes and then remove from the heat. Top with the remaining ground peanuts and bean sprouts. Garnish with coriander leaves and serve.

Glass Noodles & Stir-Fried Vegetables (Serves 6)

225g/8oz cellophane noodles (dried)
75g/3/4 cup of Chinese cabbage (shredded)
2 cloves of garlic (finely chopped)
2 small carrots (thinly sliced)
1 small stalk of celery (sliced)
4 tbsps vegetable stock
1 1/2 tbsps oyster sauce
1 tbsp fish sauce
4-5 tbsps vegetable oil
1 tsp sugar
1/4 tsp black pepper

1. Place the noodles in warm water and leave to soak for 4-5 minutes. Drain thoroughly and set aside. Heat the oil in a preheated wok and add the garlic. Cook for 2-3 minutes, until slightly golden. Add the sliced carrot and stir-fry for 2 minutes.

2. Add the stock, followed by the cabbage, celery, oyster sauce, fish sauce, sugar and black pepper; stir together well. Cook for 2 minutes. Add the noodles and toss, so that the ingredients combine well. Cook for a few minutes, until the noodles are heated through, and serve.

Noodles with Sesame Seeds & Thai Holy Basil (Serves 4)

2-3 packets of udon noodles, or rice noodles
6 cloves of garlic
1/2 cup of olive oil
2 tsp sesame oil
4 tbsps sesame seeds
3/4-1 tsp red chilli flakes
2 tbsps fish sauce
2 tbsps fresh lime juice
2 cups of Thai holy basil leaves
1 tbsp sesame seeds (lightly toasted, to garnish)

1. Cook the noodles as per the packet instructions. Place the garlic, olive oil, sesame oil, 4 tablespoons of sesame seeds, red chilli flakes, fish sauce, basil leaves and lime juice in a food processor and blend well.

2. Once blended, adjust seasonings and lime juice, if required. Drain the noodles thoroughly and return to the saucepan. Add the blended sauce and toss together well.

3. Garnish with sesame seeds. Serve immediately.

Prawn Pad Thai (Serves 4)

200g/7oz dry rice noodles (1/4 inch – soaked in tepid water for 30 minutes & drained)
20-24 large prawns (shelled & deveined)
1-2 tbsps fish sauce (according to taste)
110g/4oz water chestnuts (sliced)
100g/1 cup of fresh bean sprouts
112ml/1/2 cup of chicken stock
55g spring onions (cut into 1 inch lengths)
4 large eggs (beaten)
170ml/3/4 cup of oyster sauce
1 red chilli (finely chopped)
3 tbsps sugar
4 tbsps vinegar
2 tbsps paprika
5 tbsps crushed peanuts

1. Preheat a wok and add the prawns. Dry stir-fry for 2 minutes. Add the eggs and continue to cook, stirring continuously, until they begin to set.

2. Add the drained noodles to the wok, followed by the peanuts, paprika, water chestnuts and sugar. Mix together well and stir-fry for 2-3 minutes, until the noodles have softened.

3. Stir in the oyster sauce, vinegar and fish sauce, according to taste. Add the spring onions, chilli, stock and bean sprouts and stir-fry for 1-2 minutes; combing all of the ingredients well.

Transfer to a serving dish and serve immediately.

Rice Noodles with Seafood & Vegetables (Serves 4-6)
400g/14oz dried white rice noodles (1cm wide, soaked overnight & drained)
550g/1 lb 4oz mixed seafood; squid, cod, large prawns (all prepared)
500ml/2 1/4 cups of fish stock
350g/3 1/2 cups of Chinese kale (stalk chopped & top leaves separated)
5 cloves of garlic (finely chopped)
1 tbsp oyster sauce
1 tbsp black bean sauce
2 tbsps light soy sauce
2 tbsps cornflour
2 1/2 tbsps vegetable oil

1. Place the oyster sauce, black bean sauce, fish stock and cornflour in a bowl and mix together well.

2. Heat 1 tablespoon of the vegetable oil in a wok and add the rice noodles. Stir-fry for 4-5 minutes, until cooked through. Remove from the wok and transfer to a warm dish. Keep warm.

3. Heat the remaining oil in the wok and add the garlic. Stir-fry for 2-3 minutes. Add the seafood and chopped kale stalk and stir-fry for 4 minutes.

4. Add the combined sauce mixture and the top leaves of the kale to the wok and mix well. Stir-fry for a further 1-2 minutes and then remove from the heat. Season with white pepper, according to taste. Serve.

Steamed Chicken Rice (Serves 6)
620g/2 3/4 cups of rice (uncooked)
6 chicken breasts (skinless & cut into strips)
4 cloves of garlic
1.5 ltrs of chicken stock
1 1/2 tbsps chopped coriander root
4-5 tbsps vegetable oil
1 1/2 tsps ground white pepper
Sliced cucumber (to garnish)
Fresh coriander leaves (chopped
– to garnish)

1. Heat the vegetable oil in
a large wok and add the
garlic. Stir-fry for 2-3
minutes, until golden brown.

2. Add the chicken slices, coriander root and white pepper; stir-fry for 6-8 minutes until the chicken is cooked through. Remove the chicken with a slotted spoon and set aside, keeping it warm.

3. Add the rice to the flavoured oil in the wok and stir-fry for 3-4 minutes. Add the chicken stock and simmer gently, until the liquid is level with the surface of the rice.

4. Cover the wok, turn off the heat and leave to stand for 10-12 minutes, until all of the liquid has been absorbed.

5. Remove the lid and fluff with a fork. Spoon the rice out onto individual serving plates and top with the sliced chicken. Garnish with sliced cucumber and chopped coriander.

Serve immediately.

Steamed Sticky Rice
500g/2 1/4 cups of sticky rice

1. Soak the rice in a bowl of cold water for 3-4 hours. Drain thoroughly and transfer to a bamboo basket, lined with a double thickness muslin cloth. Spread the rice out in the basket evenly.

2. Bring a saucepan of water to the boil and set the bamboo basket over the top of the water, (taking care not to burn your hands on the steam).

3. Reduce the heat to a simmer, cover and steam for 25 minutes, until the rice is tender and swelled. Add more water during cooking, as required.

4. Once the rice is cooked, transfer to a tray and spread out, allowing the rice to cool quickly and not go soggy.

Serve immediately.

Thai Egg Noodles (Serves 4)
500g/19oz egg noodles
2 tsps peeled & finely grated galangal
3-4 birds-eye red chillies (finely chopped)
Juice of 1 1/2 limes
2 tsps clear honey
2 tsps sesame seeds
4 tsps soy sauce
2 tsps sesame oil
2 tsps fresh coriander (chopped)
3 tsps fresh holy basil (chopped)

1. Cook the egg noodles, as per the packet instructions. Whilst the noodles are cooking, place the remaining ingredients in a large bowl and combine together well.

2. Drain the cooked noodles thoroughly and return to the saucepan. Add the sauce and toss, coating the noodles well.

Transfer to a large serving dish and serve immediately.

Thai Festive Rice (Serves 4)
Rice:
225g/1 cup of jasmine rice (rinsed with cold, running water & drained)
200ml/2/3 cup of coconut milk
1 clove of garlic (crushed)
1 onion (thinly sliced)

Thai Festive Rice/cont.
1 lemon grass stalk (bruised)
375ml/1 & 2/3 cups of water
1 tbsp vegetable oil
1/4 tsp ground turmeric

Accompaniments:
Prawn crackers
Tomato wedges
Cucumber wedges
Fried onions
Fresh red chillies (shredded)

1. Heat the vegetable oil in a large frying pan and add the onions, garlic and turmeric. Cook over a gentle heat for 2-3 minutes, until the onions are tender.

2. Add the rice, stirring it well, coating it evenly in the flavoured oil. Add the coconut milk, water and lemon grass and bring to the boil, stirring continuously.

3. Reduce the heat, cover the pan and simmer for 10-12 minutes, or until the liquids have been absorbed. Remove from the heat.

4. Lift the lid from the pan and cover the top with a clean tea-towel. Replace the lid and leave to stand for 13-15 minutes.

5. Remove the lid and cloth and discard the lemon grass. Transfer the rice to a round serving platter and shape into a cone-shaped mound.

6. Surround the rice with the accompaniments and serve immediately.

Curries

Green Bean Curry (Serves 6)

600g/4 cups of French beans (cut into 2inch pieces)
180ml/3/4 cup of coconut milk
3 spring onions (sliced)
1 clove of garlic (crushed)
1 red chilli (deseeded & finely chopped)
1 tsp paprika
3 tsps Thai fish sauce
2 tbsps vegetable oil
1 lemon grass stalk (finely chopped)

1. Cook the sliced French beans in boiling water for 2-3 minutes and then drain. Keep to one side.

2. Place the chilli, paprika, coconut milk, fish sauce, garlic and lemon grass in a food processor and blend into a smooth paste.

3. Heat the vegetable oil in a preheated wok and add the chopped spring onions. Stir-fry for 1-2 minutes and then add the blended paste, then bring to the boil.

4. Reduce the heat and simmer for 4-5 minutes, reducing the liquid down. Add the beans and simmer for a further 2-3 minutes, until tender. Remove from the heat.

Serve immediately.

Green Chicken Curry (Serves 4-6)

450g/1 lb chicken breast & thigh (cubed)
395ml/1 3/4 cups of coconut milk
220g/1 1/4 cup of new potatoes (halved)
150g/2 cups of green beans (trimmed & halved)
2 cloves of garlic (finely chopped)
4 tsps Thai green curry paste
2 fresh kaffir lime leaves (finely chopped)
2 tsps Thai fish sauce
1 tsp caster sugar
1 tbsp vegetable oil
Handful of basil leaves (chopped)

1. Place the potatoes into a pan of boiling water and cook for 4-5 minutes. Add the green beans and cook for 3 minutes. Drain and set aside.

2. Heat the vegetable oil in a preheated wok and add the garlic. Cook for about 1 minute, until golden brown. Add the Thai green curry paste and stir in for 20-30 seconds. Add the coconut milk and bring to a simmer.

3. Stir in the sugar and fish sauce, followed by the cubed chicken. Cover and simmer gently for 8-10 minutes, until cooked through.

4. Add the previously cooked potatoes and green beans and cook for 1-2 minutes, heating them through. Stir in the kaffir lime leaves and basil leaves. Remove from the heat.

5. Transfer to a serving dish and serve immediately with hot rice.

Green Prawn Curry (Serves 6)

600g/1 lb 5oz frozen, cooked tiger prawns (defrosted)
150g/2/3 cup of baby spinach leaves
560ml/2 1/4 cups of canned coconut milk
3 tbsp Thai green curry paste
Juice of 1 lime
1-1 1/2 tbsps Thai fish sauce
2-3 tsps sugar
Handful of fresh coriander leaves & stalks

1. Pour the coconut milk into a serving jug, reserving the thick cream around the sides and at the base of the cans.

2. Spoon the thick coconut cream into a food processor, with 4-5 tbsps of the coconut milk. Add the coriander stalks; curry paste and sugar and blend until smooth.

3. Add the paste to a preheated wok and cook, stirring continuously, for 1-2 minutes. Pour in the rest of the coconut milk and bring just to the boil.

4. Reduce the heat to a simmer and add the prawns and spinach. Cook for 2-3 minutes, until the prawns are heated through.

5. Stir in the fish sauce and lime juice, mixing thoroughly. Adjust the fish sauce, according to taste. Remove from the heat.

6. Shred the coriander leaves and sprinkle over the top. Serve immediately over hot rice or noodles.

Massaman Beef & Potato Curry (Serves 2-4)
775g/1 lb 11oz rump steak (cut into 2 inch cubes)
265g/1 1/2 cups of potatoes (cut into 1 inch cubes)
2 medium onions (quartered)
50g/2oz massaman curry paste
180ml/3/4 cup of coconut milk (+ a little more)
395ml/1 3/4 cups of beef stock
75g/1/2 cup of roasted peanuts
2 cinnamon sticks
2 tbsps fish sauce
2 tbsps palm sugar
8 cardamom seeds
4 star anises
3 tbsps lemon juice
5 whole cloves
1 1/2 tbsps vegetable oil
1 long red chilli (deseeded & finely sliced – to garnish)

Massaman Beef & Potato Curry/cont.

1. Add the cloves, star anises; cardamom pods and cinnamon stick to a wok and dry-fry over a low heat for 2-3 minutes, until fragrant. Remove from the wok and set aside.

2. Heat the vegetable oil in the wok and add the massaman curry paste; stir-fry over a medium heat for 2-3 minutes, until fragrant.

3. Add the beef cubes and cook for 3-4 minutes. Add the beef stock, onions, coconut milk, lemon juice, fish sauce, roasted peanuts, palm sugar and dry-fried spices.

4. Bring to the boil. Reduce the heat and simmer for 20 minutes. Add the potato chunks and continue to simmer over a gentle heat for 25-30 minutes.

5. Remove from the heat and transfer to a serving bowl. Garnish with the sliced red chillies and serve immediately.

Pumpkin & Sweet Potato Curry (Serves 4-6)

500g/1 lb 2oz pumpkin (deseeded & diced)
275g sweet potato (peeled & diced)
125g/1 1/4 cups of chestnut mushrooms (sliced)
125g/1 cup of roasted peanuts (chopped)
335ml/1 1/2 cups of coconut milk
395ml/1 1/4 cups of hot vegetable stock
3 cloves of garlic (crushed)
4 shallots (finely chopped)
1 inch of fresh galangal (finely chopped)
2 tbsps vegetable oil
2 tbsps Thai fish sauce
2 tbsps yellow curry paste
1 tbsp soy sauce
3 kaffir lime leaves (shredded)
55g/2oz pumpkin seeds (toasted)

To be cooked in a slow cooker.

1. Heat the vegetable oil in a large frying pan and add the shallots and garlic. Cook for 8-10 minutes, over a medium heat, until lightly browned.

2. Stir in the yellow curry paste and stir-fry for 30-40 seconds. Transfer the mixture into the slow cooker's ceramic pot.

3. Add the galangal, sweet potatoes, pumpkin and lime leaves to the pot, followed by half of the coconut milk. Gently stir the ingredients together, combining them well. Cover and cook on a high setting for 1 1/2 hours.

4. Add the mushrooms, Thai fish sauce, soy sauce and chopped peanuts to the curry; stirring them in well. Pour in the remaining coconut milk and re-cover. Cook on high for 2 1/2-3 hours, until all the vegetables are tender.

5. Serve in bowls, garnished with a sprinkling of pumpkin seeds.

Red Beef Curry (Serves 4)
450g/2 cups of beef (sliced into strips)
750ml/3 & 1/3 cup of beef stock
88g/1/2 cup of courgette (chopped)
4 tbsps Thai red curry paste
1 tsp ground cumin
1 tsp ground coriander
1 tbsp fish sauce
2 pieces of galangal
1 tbsp dried krachai (optional)
1 tbsp dried Kaffir lime leaves
1/2 tsp sugar
2 tbsps fresh basil (finely chopped)

1. Soak the galangal in cold water for 4-5 minutes and slice. Soak the krachai in warm water for 25-30 minutes and finely slice.

2. Pour 115ml/1/2 cup of the beef stock into a saucepan and bring to the boil. Stir in the red curry paste, cumin, coriander, lime leaves, galangal and krachai. Stir well, combining all the ingredients.

Red Beef Curry/cont.

3. Add the remaining stock and bring back to the boil. Stir in the beef strips and fish sauce, reduce the heat and simmer for 4-5 minutes, until tender. Stir in the sugar and taste; add a little more fish sauce if needed.

4. Add the chopped courgette and simmer for 2-3 minutes. Remove from the heat and stir in the chopped basil. Serve with rice.

Red Lamb Curry (Serves 4)

525g/1 lb 3oz lamb leg (diced)
395ml/1 3/4 cups of coconut milk
110g/3/4 cup unsalted cashew nuts (finely chopped)
250g/9oz baby new potatoes (halved lengthways)
1 1/2 tbsps Thai red curry paste
1-1 1/2 tbsps Thai fish sauce
2 kaffir lime leaves (crumbled)
1 tbsp tomato puree
1 tbsp brown sugar
1 tbsp groundnut oil
Lime wedges (to serve)

1. Heat the groundnut oil in a wok and stir in the curry paste. Cook for 1 minute over a high heat. Add the lamb and cook for 3-4 minutes, stirring frequently.

2. Add the coconut milk, cashew nuts, lime leaves and tomato puree, combining well. Bring to the boil. Reduce the heat and simmer for 50-60 minutes, until thickened, stirring occasionally.

3. Whilst the lamb is simmering, cook the potato halves in boiling water for 8-10 minutes, until just tender. Drain and set aside.

4. Towards the end of the lamb's cooking time, add the potatoes and cook for a further 5-8 minutes. Serve immediately with hot rice, garnished with lime wedges for squeezing.

Seafood Curry (Serves 6)
750g/1 lb 11oz halibut (cut into chunks)
300g/11oz squid (cleaned, tentacles removed)
18 fresh clams (in shells, cleaned)
300g/11oz tiger prawns (raw, peeled & deveined)
6 shallots (finely chopped)
3 tbsps Thai green curry paste
1 1/2 tbsps vegetable oil
2 cloves of garlic (crushed)
1 1/2 tsps shrimp paste
750ml/3 & 1/3 cups of coconut milk
8 fresh basil leaves (finely shredded)

1. Cut the squid body 'shells' into thick rings. Heat the vegetable oil in a preheated wok and add the garlic, shallots and curry paste. Stir-fry for 2-3 minutes.

2. Stir in the shrimp paste and add the coconut milk; bring to the boil. Reduce the heat to a simmer and add the prawns, squid and halibut; simmer for 2-3 minutes.

3. Add the clams in their shells and simmer for 1-2 minutes, until the clams open. Remove any clamshells, which fail to open. Remove from the heat and stir in the basil leaves.

Serve with hot rice.

Sweet Thai Red Pork Curry (Serves 6)

750g/1 lb 11oz pork (sliced into strips)
4 tbsps vegetable oil
750ml/3 & 1/3 cups of coconut milk
4 tbsps Thai red curry paste
3 tbsps fish sauce
75g/3oz bamboo shoots
1 1/2 tsps dried Kaffir lime leaves
1 1/2 tsps sugar
1/2 tsp fresh chilli (finely chopped)
1 tbsp fresh basil (finely chopped)

1. Soak the lime leaves in cold water for 8-10 minutes and slice. Heat the vegetable oil in a wok and add the red curry paste, stir-fry over a low/medium heat for 2-3 minutes.

2. Add 130ml of the coconut milk and the lime leaves. Simmer gently for 3-4 minutes, stirring frequently. Add the pork strips and cook for 4-5 minutes, until the sauce begins to thicken.

3. Add the remaining coconut milk, the fish sauce and sugar and cook until the pork is cooked. A few minutes before serving add the fresh chilli and bamboo shoots. Cook for 2-3 minutes, remove from the heat and stir in the basil.

Serve with rice.

Thai Salmon Curry (Serves 4-6)
500g/1 lb 2oz salmon fillet (skinless, deboned & cut into 1 inch chunks)
450ml/2 cups of hot vegetable stock (or chicken)
1 tbsp Thai fish sauce
2 cloves of garlic (crushed)
3 shallots (finely chopped)
3/4 tsp dried chilli flakes
1 lemon grass stalk (finely chopped)
1 inch pieces of fresh root ginger (finely chopped)
1 tsp light muscovado sugar

To be cooked in a slow cooker.

1. Place the salmon chunks in a bowl, cover and leave to stand at room temperature.

2. Turn the slow cooker to a high temperature and add the hot stock. Add the ginger, lemon grass, sugar, fish sauce, garlic, shallots and chilli flakes and combine well.

3. Cover the slow cooker and cook for 2-2 1/4 hours. Add a little more stock, if required.

4. Add the salmon chunks to the slow cooker. Re-cover and cook for 12-15 minutes. Turn the slow cooker off and leave the curry in the pot for a further 15 minutes, until the salmon is cooked through.

Serve immediately in serving bowls.

Black Bean Curry (Serves 4)

500g/1 lb 2oz black beans (soaked overnight and drained)
395g/1 3/4 cups of chopped, canned tomatoes
3 celery sticks (chopped)
2 onions (sliced)
4 cloves of garlic (crushed)
1 tsp chilli powder
1 cm piece of root ginger (finely chopped)
2 tsps ground cumin
2 tsps ground coriander
1 tsp cardamom seeds
1 tsp chilli powder
3 tbsps vegetable oil
1 tsp garam masala
1 tbsp fresh coriander leaves (chopped)
Salt (to season)

1. Place the drained beans in a pan and cover with cold water. Bring to the boil and boil rapidly for 10 minutes. Reduce the heat, cover and simmer for 1-1 1/2 hours, until tender. Add a pinch of salt towards the end of the cooking time. Drain the beans, reserving 300ml/1 1/4 cups of the liquid.

2. Heat the vegetable oil in a saucepan and add the onions, cook for 3-4 minutes, until softened. Stir in the garam masala, cumin, ground coriander, chilli powder, ginger, garlic and cook for 1 minute, stirring continuously.

3. Add the reserved liquid to the saucepan, followed by the chopped tomatoes, beans, celery and cardamom seeds. Season with salt, according to taste. Bring to the boil and then reduce the heat, cover and simmer for 40-45 minutes.

4. Remove from the heat and stir in the chopped coriander leaves.

Serve immediately with hot rice.

Thai Spinach and Potato Curry (Serves 6)

300g/11oz baby spinach leaves
375g/13oz potato (cut into 2cm chunks)
150ml vegetable stock
2 cloves of garlic
300ml coconut milk
1 onion (sliced into thin rings)
3 tsps Thai red curry paste
3/4 tsp ground turmeric
5 tbsps vegetable oil
1 1/2 tsps coriander seeds
1 stalk of lemon grass (finely chopped)
1 1/2 inch of fresh root ginger (finely chopped)

1. Grind the ginger, garlic, coriander seeds and chopped lemon grass in a mortar and pound with a pestle, until a smooth paste – or, mix in a spice grinder.

2. Heat 3 tbsps of the vegetable oil in a preheated wok and stir in the paste mixture. Stir-fry for 20-30 seconds. Stir in the turmeric and curry paste, mixing the ingredients together well.

3. Pour in the coconut milk and bring to the boil. Pour in the vegetable stock and add the potatoes; bring back to the boil.

4. Reduce the heat and simmer for 10-12 minutes. Add the spinach, stirring it through and simmer for a couple of minutes, until wilted. Remove from the heat.

5. About halfway through the curry's simmering time, heat the remaining vegetable oil in a frying pan and add the onion rings. Cook for 4-6 minutes, until golden and crispy.

6. Transfer the curry into a serving dish and top with the onion. Serve immediately.

Yellow Chicken Curry (Serves 2-4)
2 tbsps Thai yellow curry paste
325g/12oz chicken breast (skinless & thinly sliced)
225ml/1 cup of chicken stock
180ml/3/4 cup of coconut milk (well shaken)
300g/1 1/2 cups of fresh pineapple (cut into 1 inch cubes)
1 long red chilli (deseeded & finely chopped – to garnish)
1 tbsp vegetable oil
1 1/2-2 tbsps fish sauce

1. Heat the vegetable oil in a wok and add the yellow curry paste. Stir-fry for 2-3 minutes, until fragrant.

2. Add the chicken slices and stir-fry for 5-6 minutes. Add the stock, coconut milk, pineapple chunks and 1 1/2 tablespoons of the fish sauce. Cook for 2 minutes, stirring continuously.

3. Taste and add more fish sauce if required. Remove from the heat and spoon into a serving bowl. Garnish with the chopped chillies and serve immediately.

Curries

Desserts

Bananas in Black Sticky Rice (Serves 4)

100g/1/2 cup of dried black beans (soaked overnight)
170g/3/4 cup of glutinous rice (soaked overnight, rinsed & drained)
275g/10oz coconut cream
2 tbsps sugar
2 bananas (halved)
4 banana leaf
Pinch of salt

1. Boil the black beans until tender, as per the package instructions. Set aside.

2. Place the sugar, coconut cream and a pinch of salt in a bowl and combine together well.

3. Place the drained rice in a saucepan and turn the hob onto a low heat. Gradually add the coconut cream, stirring with a wooden spoon.

4. Bring to a simmer, stirring continuously, and cook until the rice is tender and all of the coconut milk has been absorbed. Remove from the heat and set aside to cool.

5. Place a portion of the cooled, cooked rice on a banana leaf and mix in a portion of black beans. Top with a banana half and then with another layer of rice and black beans.

6. Fold the leaf over the filling and tie securely with string. Repeat this process for the remaining ingredients.

7. Steam the banana parcels for 12-15 minutes and then set aside to cool.

Once cool enough, unwrap and serve.

Desserts

Banana in Coconut Milk (Serves 4)

4 bananas (only just ripe)
1 ltr coconut milk (left to stand)
75g/1/3 cup of sugar
2 tbsp palm sugar
2 drops of pandan extract (available from Asian supermarkets/stores)
Pinch of salt

1. Steam the bananas in their skins in a covered steamer, over a pan of simmering water – for about 5 minutes, until the skins begin to break.

2. Remove from the heat and leave to cool a little. Carefully peel and cut each banana into quarters, lengthways and then across.

3. Once the coconut milk has stood long enough for the thick coconut milk to rise to the surface, spoon 500ml of the top layer into a separate bowl to reserve.

4. Place the remaining coconut milk and pandan extract in a saucepan and heat over a medium/high heat. Bring to the boil and add the sugars, salt and banana chunks.

5. Add the reserved thickened coconut milk and bring back to the boil. Reduce the heat and simmer for 2-3 minutes.

6. Remove from the heat and serve in individual serving bowls. Can be eaten hot or cold.

Black Sticky Rice Pudding (Serves 8)

450g/2 cups of black sticky rice
500ml/2 cups of coconut cream
60ml/3/4 cup of coconut cream
115g/1/2 cup of sugar
1.8 ltrs water

1. Place the sticky rice and water in a large saucepan and place over a medium/high heat. Bring to the boil.

2. Reduce the heat and simmer for about 30 minutes, stirring occasionally to begin with and more frequently towards to the end of cooking time. Add more water if required.

3. Once the rice is just tender, add the sugar and 500ml/2 1/4 cups of the coconut cream. Combine well, whilst continuing to cook for a few more minutes.

4. Remove from the heat and spoon into individual serving bowls. Serve immediately with a little more coconut cream drizzled over the top.

Coconut Custard Squares (Serves 6)
10 eggs (beaten)
750ml/3 cups of thick coconut milk
170g/3/4 cup of brown sugar
3 tbsp desiccated coconut
1 tbsp rosewater

1. Preheat the oven to 180C/350F/Gas mark 5. Grease a large shallow rectangular baking dish.

2. Place all of the ingredients in a large bowl and beat together. Place the bowl over a saucepan of simmering water, stirring continuously. Cook until the mixture resembles a soft scrambled eggs consistency.

3. Pour into the greased baking dish and place in the oven for 25-30 minutes. Remove from the oven and preheat the grill to a medium setting.

4. Place the baking dish under the grill for a couple of minutes, until lightly golden. Remove and leave to cool.

Once cooled, refrigerate for at least 2 hours.

Cut into squares to serve.

Coconut Ice Cream (Serves 4)

310ml/1 1/4 cups of thick coconut milk
375ml/1 1/2 cups of fresh cream
150g/2/3 cup of sugar
2 eggs
2 egg yolks
1 tsp vanilla
1/2 tsp salt
50g/2oz sweetened, shredded coconut (dry-dried until golden)
Fresh mint sprigs

1. Place the coconut milk and cream in a saucepan and heat over a medium temperature; heat for a few minutes, taking care not to boil or burn the mixture.

2. Place the 2 eggs and 2 yolks in a bowl and beat together. Add the sugar, vanilla and salt and beat in well.

3. Pour the egg mixture into a bowl and place over a saucepan of simmering water. Gradually beat in the warm coconut milk/cream mixture, adding a little at a time. Stir continuously until the mixture thickens enough to coat the back of the spoon.

4. Remove from heat and leave to cool, stirring occasionally.

5. Spoon out evenly into a metal tray and place in the freezer for 1 1/2-2 hours, until half frozen.

6. Remove from the freezer and scoop out into a large bowl. Beat the mixture until smooth and then return to the metal tray.

7. Repeat this process once more, before covering the ice-cream and returning it to the freezer to freeze completely.

8. When ready to serve, remove from the freezer for 10 minutes before serving. Spoon into individual bowls and garnish with shredded coconut and fresh mint.

Fresh Mango Ice Cream (Serves 6)

6 ripe mangoes (peeled, seeded & cut into chunks)
280g/1 1/4 cups of sugar
560ml/2 1/4 cups of double cream (whipped until stiff)
1 1/2 tbsps lemon juice
1 1/2 tbsps gelatine (dissolved in 4 1/2 tbsps water)
Extra mango slices (to garnish)
6 fresh mint sprigs (to garnish)

1. Place the mango chunks in a bowl and add the lemon juice, sugar and dissolved gelatine; combine together until well mixed and the sugar has dissolved.

2. Carefully fold the whipped cream into the mango mixture. Spoon out evenly into a metal tray and place in the freezer for 1 1/2-2 hours, until half frozen.

3. Remove from the freezer and scoop out into a large bowl. Beat the mixture until smooth and then return to the metal tray.

4. Repeat this process once more, before covering the ice-cream and returning it to the freezer to freeze completely.

5. When ready to serve, remove from the freezer for 10 minutes before serving. Spoon into individual bowls and garnish with fresh mango slices and a sprig of fresh mint.

Orange in Rose Syrup (Serves 4)

4 oranges (peeled, pith removed & separated into segments)
375ml/1 & 2/3 cups of water
1 tsp rosewater
225g/1 cup of sugar

1. Place the orange segments in a glass serving bowl and set aside.

2. Place the sugar and water in a saucepan and bring to a gentle boil, stirring frequently. Simmer for 15-20 minutes, until a thin syrup-like thickness.

3. Stir in the rosewater and combine well. Pour over the orange segments and leave to cool. Refrigerate for 1-2 hours and then serve.

Red Ruby Dessert (Serves 2-4)

375ml/1 1/2 cups of coconut milk
95g/3/4 cup of tapioca flour
225ml/1 cup of water chestnuts (cut into 1cm cubes)
395ml/1 3/4 cups of water
115g/1/2 cup of sugar
2 tbsps sugar (dissolved in 85ml hot water)
1/2 tsp red food colouring
1 1/4 tsp salt

1. Place the sugar/water mixture in a bowl and set aside. Place the water chestnut cubes in a bowl and stir in the red food colouring. Combine well and leave to soak for 4-5 minutes.

2. Spoon the tapioca flour onto a plate and evenly coat the water chestnut cubes. Leave to sit in the flour until ready to cook.

3. Bring a large saucepan of water to the boil and add half of the water chestnuts; having shaken off any excess flour. Cook, stirring continuously, for 2-3 minutes, until translucent.

4. Whilst the water chestnuts are cooking, fill a bowl with ice cold water. Using a slotted spoon, remove the water chestnuts from the saucepan and transfer immediately to the ice cold water. Repeat this process for the remaining half of the water chestnuts.

5. Drain the water chestnuts and transfer to the bowl holding the sugar/water mixture. Set aside.

6. Place the 400ml/1 3/4 cups water and 115g/1/2 cup of sugar in a saucepan and bring to the boil. Stir in the coconut milk and heat over a medium temperature, but do not boil.

7. Add the salt and remove from the heat, stir the salt in well and leave to cool. Once cooled, cover and place in the refrigerator until chilled.

8. To serve, evenly spoon the water chestnuts into the base of a serving bowl and cover with the chilled coconut milk.

Refreshing Fruit Platter (Serves 8)
1/2 sweet, red watermelon (deseeded & flesh cut into 1/2-inch slices)
2 ripe papayas (deseeded & flesh cut into 1/2-inch chunks)
2 fresh pineapples (flesh cut into 1/2-inch chunks)
1 lime (cut into quarters)

1. Lay out each of the different fruits in alternate lines on a serving platter. Refrigerate for 30 minutes to chill.

2. Remove from the refrigerator and squeeze lime juice over the papaya before serving.

Watermelon, Orange & Ginger Sorbet (Serves 8)
3kg/6 lbs 3/4oz sweet, red watermelon (flesh deseeded & cut into cubes)
3/4 inch of fresh root ginger (peeled & finely sliced)
Juice of 2 oranges
Rind of 1 orange

1. Place the watermelon, orange juice, ginger and orange rind in a food processor and blend until smooth.

Watermelon, Orange & Ginger Sorbet/cont.

2. Transfer the mixture to a freezer-safe container, cover and freeze for 1 1/2-2 hours, until half frozen.

3. Remove from the freezer and return the mixture to the food processor. Return to the freezer container, cover and freeze again for 1 hour. Remove and blend again.

4. Repeat this process twice more during the freezing process. Cover again and return to the freezer to freeze completely.

5. Remove 5 minutes before serving and spoon into individual bowls.

Sweet Banana Pancakes (Serves 2-4)
525g/1 lb 3oz bananas (mashed)
250ml/1 cup of coconut cream
1 3/4 tbsp dried coconut
75g/2/3 cup of flour
112g/1/2 cup of sugar
1 tbsp vegetable oil
1/4 tbsp dried coconut (for garnish)

1. In a large bowl, alternately add a little of the coconut cream, dried coconut, sugar, flour and mashed banana. Beat thoroughly with a fork and then continue to add the remaining quantities of the same ingredients, until well mixed into a thick batter.

2. Heat the vegetable oil in a frying pan and pour in enough batter to make one pancake, (approx. 7 to 8cm in diameter). Cook over a medium heat for a couple of minutes, until the underneath is golden brown and the top of the pancake bubbles a little.

3. Carefully flip the pancake over and cook until golden brown. Remove from the frying pan and transfer to a plate. Keep warm whilst the remaining pancakes are cooked, or serve immediately.

Serve warm with vanilla ice-cream and a sprinkling of dried coconut.

Desserts

My Recipe

Ingredients:

Preparation:

My Recipe

Ingredients:

Preparation:

My Recipe

Ingredients:

Preparation:

My Recipe

Ingredients:

Preparation:

My Recipe

Ingredients:

Preparation:

My Recipe

Ingredients:

Preparation:

Index and
Conversions

index

Index

Spoons to millilitres

1/2 Teaspoon	2.5ml	1 Tablespoon	15ml
1 Teaspoon	5ml	2 Tablespoons	30ml
1-1/2 Teaspoons	7.5ml	3 Tablespoons	45ml
2 Teaspoons	10 ml	4 Tablespoons	60ml

Grams to Ounces

10g	0.25oz	225g	8oz
15g	0.38oz	250g	9oz
25g	1oz	275g	10oz
50g	2oz	300g	11oz
75g	3oz	350g	12oz
110g	4oz	375g	13oz
150g	5oz	400g	14oz
175g	6oz	425g	15oz
200g	7oz	450g	16oz

Metric to Cups

Flour etc	115g	1 cup
Clear Honey etc	350g	1 cup
Liquids	225ml	1 cup

Liquid measures

5fl oz	1/4 pint	150ml
7.5fl oz		215ml
10fl oz	1/2 pint	275ml
15fl oz		425ml
20fl oz	1 pint	570ml
35fl oz	1-3/4 pints	1 litre

Temperature

Celsius	Farenheit	Gas Mark	Description
110c	225F	1/4	very cool
130c	250F	1/2	very cool
140c	275F	1	cool
150c	300F	2	cool
170c	325F	3	very moderate
180c	350F	4	moderate
190c	375F	5	moderate
200c	400F	6	moderately hot
220c	425F	7	hot
230c	450F	8	hot
240c	475F	9	very hot

Conversions